OPTIMISM

In the Age of Reset

Tony B. Wolf

Dedicated to Generation **Z**

Would the world be a better place if the human species could make better decisions?

And where does it start?

This story follows the development path of an analyst and product designer who identifies a product that can be used by all humans that want to become wiser.

Any coincidences with anything at all are coincidental.

KP
Korsgaard Publishing
ISBN: 978-87-93987-48-7.
Copyright 2022 © Tony B. Wolf.
All rights reserved.
www.InTheAgeOfReset.com
www.KorsgaardPublishing.com
Wolf@IntheAgeOfReset.com
First edition 2022.

TABLE OF CONTENTS

PRELUDE

The epochal year 2020 introduced a global, co-ordinated event. We were warned, however. Authors approved of by the establishment have written about it in white papers, presentations, and books dating as far back as the 1970s.

Every time the economic system is broken, there are significant social maneuvers taking place before the actual collapse enters the public consciousness. Big systems create the conditions in which whatever chosen agenda can move forward, but such systems cannot act on a day-to-day basis.

By June 2020, we learned of a new future in store for all of us: A future without private property, a future where personal liberties are dramatically curtailed with the aid of digital tools, restrictive legislations, and total propaganda. The so-called "new normal" makes anything else look pale in comparison.

The quality of life, as we used to know it, will be significantly exacerbated in the months and years to come. Diseases, the destruction of the "just-in-time" production, and the supply chain cycle releasing the conditions of hyper-inflation upon the general public – combined with never ending mandates – will restrict and change everything we considered as part of life, not to mention climate change. All of these, plus the influx of wars, will make it much harder to survive.

Surrounded and constantly bombarded by bad news, be they real or manufactured, the question that comes to the mind of a classic philosopher is – is there anything left to be optimistic about? Obviously those seeking a better future will have to re-adjust and adapt to the newly introduced trends and conditions, which determine and dictate our lives in more and more areas every day.

Optimism in the Age of Reset presents one of the directions where Optimism can be found.

Written in 2012, this book has more relevance and appeal now than ever before.

CHAPTER 1: HIGH HOPES

(1993)

Hope in reality is the worst of all evils because it prolongs the torments of man.
Friedrich Nietzsche

Georgetown, Washington D.C. is known for its red-brick architecture. Georgetown University is world-known for the quality of education it provides, and, on this particular day, it is graduation day. The graduates of political sciences and international affairs enjoy their well-deserved minutes of initial fame. In the great university hall, one of the world's leading living historians, Professor Wunderberg addresses the audience. "Dear students and parents. Welcome to Georgetown University. Let us enjoy this day of graduation. Our students have shown traditional qualities of seeking knowledge and debating in the manner of old democracies. Now comes the time when our students will enter the lives of the working people and contribute to the societies they come from. Students from all corners of the world study at Georgetown, and we do our best to return this trust with top quality knowledge we have to offer. It is 1993, and at the end of the 20th century, many questions remain open. As an increasingly global society, we share the same concerns and hopes. The 20th century brought us two World Wars, in which probably a hundred million people perished. Historians claim that the total casualty list of the wars fought in this century may be two hundred million dead, while the economic damage, lost opportunities and the misery are not expressed nor accounted for. We are happy that the Cold War that followed the World Wars, with the United States of America and the Soviet Union as their visible proponents came to an end. Mutual Assured Destruction of the planet will not happen. Just a few years ago, both super powers, combined, had amassed almost 70,000 nuclear warheads. In all of known history, never did mankind possess such a devastating destructive potential. It is a time of high hopes. It is the time when science and technology increasingly provide us with solutions to many of our problems. We can actually feed billions of people, and provide them with clothing and better medical services. It is a time of great opportunity, and it remains a time of great uncertainty. At the advent of the 21st century, it is our hope that the world of humans will find more reasons to come together than to stay apart. We learn that there are some new challenges ahead of us, not only the questions of overpopulation, but also the impact of our way of life upon the climate of our planet. Events seem to be increasing, yet it all could just be an illusion due to the coverage of events made possible by modern technology. The true dangers and challenges lie within the human being. This generation of graduates is entering a different world where the challenges will be greater than a generation ago. The economy will more than ever before be the dominant and most important issue concerning all of us.

The world is rapidly becoming more and more competitive. Old tradecrafts are dying out so quickly that new technologically-enabled tradecrafts are not filling the vacuum. Even the best and brightest of the world's analysts have a hard time estimating where the planet will be in 2020. I know this, by 2020, all of you graduates will enter the time in which you will hold some power in your hands. And we hope that the education you received with us will help you make sound decisions. Many of you will become administrators in the governments of the countries you come from, some will turn to journalism, while others will end up as boring professors, and some will, in time, rise to positions of real political power. Such is the tradition and nature of the topic you graduated. Graduates of political sciences and international affairs, I wish you all the best in the times ahead."

Students, professors, parents, guests, all mingled and socialized after the professor ended his speech. One student had nobody to attend his graduation, so it seemed. Professor Wunderberg asked the young graduate to meet someone who came to this graduation with the purpose of recruiting one particular student. The three men met in the cozy office of the professor; it was a room filled with books, manuscripts, and papers.

THE OPPORTUNITY

"Gentleman, I am the only person familiar to all in this room, yes? So, let me get to the point. This young graduate is Mr. Sol, his full name being Viktor Sol; he is a typical European mixture of genes and history. He was born in 1969 and comes from what is known as Central Europe. Inheriting some small property from his grandparents, Sol used it to finance the start of the education he was interested in, here at Georgetown University. As some students do, he had several jobs that helped him finish his studies, plus, he received a nice scholarship for the second half of his education. I consider Sol as one of the brightest students, which I have had in the recent years. I also know that Sol does not come from a privileged social background, thus, a job working as an administrator is not likely to be his career choice. The gentleman with a hat, this is Mr. Max. He is the Chairman of the board of directors of a private scientific institution, or better to say a think tank from Switzerland. The name of the institution is simple: the Institute. They are not in the yellow pages; they need not advertise their work. They are the real deal for insiders and have been in this particular business since 1919. Mr. Max and the Institute extended the scholarship you received, Sol. And they did so, because they trust my judgment and you were my choice. Both as a bright student in the need of a scholarship as well as a bright student who may, in time and with training become a wise analyst."

"Thank you professor for the introduction, I'd like to expand on your thoughts, the gentleman will understand, I have business to attend these days, thus, no time to waste. Sol, I am pleased to meet you. We have been working with the professor for now thirty years. He has always been a very reliable and trustworthy associate. The fact that he also received numerous international awards for his work in history, only underlines this. A few words about what we do. The Institute was founded in the spring of 1919. The inspiration came from the horrors of the First World War, which was the collective suicide of the then European powers that brought an abrupt end to several empires and created some new nation states or at least experimented with it. It also introduced the United States to the world as a power that others will have to reckon with in the 20th century. The founder of the Institute was an ancestor of mine who lived through the trench warfare and personally felt all the misery, the inhumane conditions in which humanity may end up. Having served on the Western front in 1917 and 1918, he lost two thirds of the men under his command. My ancestor's idea, at least then, was to bring some bright minds together and provide non-biased, neutral opinion to the politicians in order to prevent another slaughter like the First World War. Since Switzerland has a long tradition of neutrality, he brought his idea to life in the area around Zurich. When any war ends, humans tend to have high hopes for the future, because they are humble. One is humble after having lived through hard times. This is how the establishment known as the Institute was born."

Mr. Max paused and observed Sol who sat quietly. Then he continued:

"The people in the Institute put together historical knowledge and combine it with human nature, and the process of decision-making in order to see the possible future outcome. Like a crystal ball. But it is all mathematics, correlations between different factors, a vast database of past historical situations and thousands of man/days of hard analytic work that make it possible to foresee the possible outcomes of any situation. Way back then, they had no computers; it was all papers and pens. The optimism of the generation that experienced war merged with the increasing efficiency of machines. These were still the times of the advanced phases of the Western industrial revolution. In the 1920s, in the US but also other places, optimism was immense. People started to enjoy the benefits of peace; some economies introduced the credit line and people could buy things they need on credit, with perhaps 10% of the value down paid. At some moment in the 1920s, the United States amassed so much extra cash from their worldwide exports that it was incomprehensible not to believe in endless growth. During the 1920s, the Institute did some work for various governments, which helped the Institute grow. Then, in the late 1920s the overcapacity of the world's production lines became evident.

The Institute saw the possible events of the future as alarming, but the politicians did not want to hear bad news. Only good news would sell, everyone believed in endless growth. In 1928, the Institute lost several of its key government clients and it seemed that my ancestor would have to look for a job. Then, a banker heard about the work the Institute did. My ancestor had either to close the shop or start providing top quality council to the private sector. A long story made short, in the following years the estimates and predictions of the Institute brought real fortunes to private investors who commissioned the Institute's services. The Great Depression brought earning opportunities, to some. As a result, the Institute became self-sufficient and my ancestor purchased land in the area around Zurich to build the infrastructure for the Institute that serves us to this day. It was an interesting period because with the Great Depression, people lost confidence in the Free Market economy. It was the time of competing ideologies. The 20th century saw many competing ideologies: Liberalism, Socialism, Marxism, Communism, Conservatism, Anarchism, Nationalism, Fascism, Corporatism, and a few more. Many of these shared one trait: centrally, rigidly governed structures that determined almost every detail and aspect of life. Eyewitnesses say that people placed high hopes on these centrally planned and run governments and, hence, economic systems. Since 1935, the Institute provides services only to the private sector. The reasoning was simple. Economic growth or economic recessions develop based upon certain conditions and actions. My ancestor considered that the basis for everything is the economy. During the carnage of the Second World War, the Institute sheltered and gave work to more than a hundred fleeing scientists and intellectuals. Some of the basic structures of our mathematical system originate from that time. In 1949, the Institute purchased the first available digital computer – ENIAC. It was a huge machine, weighing nearly 30 tons. Just a few users in the world could afford it. We invested significant sums in computing power ever since. The Institute is in business for 74 years and we are among the leaders in our field of work."

"Wow Sir. This sounds like compressed history and science fiction business combined. What is it that the Institute really does, in layman's terms?"

"We are in the wisdom business. Let me explain. A person has to make decisions on a daily basis. How does one know which decision is the right one? It takes life experience to sharpen the decision-making process in ways that most decisions are the right ones. This is called judgment. And how does one obtain good judgment? Through bad judgment – that exposes the person to bad experiences. The problem is, all of this takes time and some decisions can have a negative effect on your whole life. Individual decisions affect the individual and his family; corporate decisions affect whole systems. A decision maker, responsible for one hundred thousand paychecks, needs a far better overview of all the options and possible consequences of his decisions. Such people need decision-making and risk management tools. An opportunistic individual may survive on random jobs. You cannot expect a hundred thousand paychecks being paid every month based only on opportunity. Big systems cannot function on a day-by-day basis like individuals can. The Institute does comprehensive analysis of all the possible variables, and it provides the clients with executive summaries to any question of their interest. Our clients know that bad decisions can lead to ruin; thus, they are not interested in wishful thinking. Our clients appreciate our work because we provide them with factual analysis. Almost any question and situation can be analyzed and future projections can be made quite accurately. Some call this process forecasting. By definition, forecasting is the ability to predict and, therefore, influence future events as a result of forecasted knowledge."

"Mr. Max, thank you for your explanation. What did I do to deserve your interest and the scholarship? What is it that I may do for you in the future?"

"We require smart and hardworking analysts in different fields of human knowledge. These people work as teams aided by some of the strongest computing and data storage capacities and provide the final product to our clients. I read your essay about accidental nuclear warfare, and a theoretical technology that may prevent accidental outbreak of nuclear war due to human error. It was a good essay, showing the cohesion of mind and technology in the search for solutions. So you got your scholarship. We do not need idealistic youth; we need young people who have the zeal, to help us do our job professionally. If you are interested, we offer you a fixed employment contract and a place to live and work in Switzerland. The salary is not huge but is solid. For some people, it is interesting work. If you decide to take this chance, there is a five-month internship followed by a three-month definitional mission. If you don't want the job after you've gone through the definitional mission, we let you go and you pay back the scholarship in some reasonable time-frame. How does that sound to you, Sol?"

"It sounds thrilling, Sir. A job as an administrator is not exactly what I can afford."

"Thank Professor Wunderberg. Meet me tomorrow in front of the Smithsonian Natural History museum at 1400 hours. We need to make the best out of the available time."

THE CONVERSATION

The Washington National Mall gives a special touch to D.C. The National Mall, as an open area National Park, serves government employees, D.C. citizens, tourists visiting the capital and business men alike, and it is surrounded by a range of Museums.

"Good afternoon Mr. Max, this is a great place to meet. I spend many hours in the various Smithsonian Museums. It is one of my favorite places to go and meditate."

"That's why they built them. My favorite is the Natural History museum; guess you are more a fan of the Air and Space Museum."

The two gentlemen walked through the exposition, exchanging thoughts.

"Sol, why did you choose to study in the U.S. and not in Europe?"

"Sir, the Virginia declaration of rights, which served as the basis for the Declaration of Independence, is my favorite event in modern times. I found the American ideals most appealing. I believe that an individual has value, and, if given the proper surrounding, an individual can contribute positively to the society whereby a society that eliminates the chances for an individual, embarks on the path of inevitable decline."

"I understand. You find inspiration in the events of 1776. There were many inspiring events in history. The 19th and 20th centuries are full of revolutions and great promises. All these events included very promising and idealistic objectives written on paper. Times change and ideals are often nothing more than high hopes."

"Sir, there are many things that are confusing, but I learned to distinguish between history and the present time following the principles of realpolitik. The world is as it is. Sometimes I still have troubles with this, but I try to see the world for what it is."

"What about manufactured history, it is practiced all around our planet. The winner writes the history. History can be a mirage. Perhaps one believes in something that actually was very different or never even existed?"

"Certainly Sir, I learned early on to be thorough in everything I do. Researching a single topic can reveal many hidden details; it is good to read various versions of the same events, preferably from different sources and in different languages."

"What about the natural way of things? People change, nations change, times change? The American revolution of the 18th century is a nice story in the background. In 1776, the 13 colonies that represented the basis for what is now the USA had perhaps 2.5 million people, not counting the indigenous tribes. Today we are galloping towards the number of 300 million citizens. Two hundred seventeen years is about nine generations. Not much is left from the time of the founding fathers."

"Sir, time definitively has influence over the developmental path of the society."

"You are a right Sol, but there are differences in how time is being perceived. Some see time happening as a linear event, and it has a start and a direction; this allows for all sorts of future promises to be projected. This is a good control and profit mechanism since you can sell hope. But you heard of the saying – what goes around comes around, yes? Some see time happening in cycles, events repeating themselves, thus, there is no need for hope. Instead, one prepares and adjusts to what is coming based upon past experiences. Do you know the story about the three generations?"

"Three generations?"

"Remember this story since you will find it any place because it is a human characteristic. This is how it goes. There was this titan of a man, a person capable of creating lasting wealth. He worked all of his life, started from scratch several times, swallowed pride, disciplined himself and was totally committed to the business he pursued. That is the grandfather in this story. His work, and the risks he took, created jobs for many people. Many families depended upon the work of him. His son grew up in the shadows of the titan, and he was introduced to the family business early on. He might have wanted to do other things or simply hope that his inheritance would come soon enough. But, the watchful eye of the titan was always present. Then he dies. Now his son has already past the age of 50. His youth's gone, and the influence of the titan is always there; he simply carries on the family tradition. He understands the responsibility of being in charge of the wealth. He also remembers that the family went through extreme hardships, so he protects the wealth. Now comes the time for the grandson to enter the stage. The grandson had a great childhood and received the best available education, but he does not remember how this wealth came to existence. He never knew any hardships, as there was always someone to help out and money was never a problem. The grandson inherits everything. He considers that he is the chosen one. Providence gave him a special role in life; why else would he inherit such a great fortune while billions of people inherit nothing? The grandson follows his own set of rules. Some of the wealth went on gambling and other vices. Some of it got spent on unrealistic business concepts and ideas. One day, everything is gone and the only new thing the grandson created is a lot of extra debt. There is a lesson in this old story, and you can absolutely apply this lesson to bigger entities, not just a single family. You can apply this wisdom to whole nations. It is simply a human characteristic. Do you get the picture?"

"Yes Sir, I get the picture. It is quite logical. One who did not suffer does not know the value of something because all is given to him."

"Here another question, Sol: what other document or book published in the same year as the Declaration of Independence had a much higher impact on the economy of the Western world?"

"I do not know, Sir."

"In 1776, a Scottish economist wrote a book in which he argued that economic growth has multiple blessings for the society and the people involved. He advised that economic growth should be constant, aided with increasing numbers of people, optimized organization, and process skills, as well the introduction of better machines and tools that make tasks simpler or quicker. At that time, it was Great Britain who held the biggest Empire of its time and also was the first nation to introduce the industrial revolution. This recipe of eternal and constant growth was followed by many governments around this planet. Economy was always the crucial element of any society. When the economy is good, people are in a good mood. When the economy sucks, people are susceptible of second thoughts about everything. The American Revolution was about money, and independence came as a result of these concerns. Economy is the key to everything. It is directly linked to security; if you have poor security, you cannot develop a fully functioning economy. Always remember this: economy and security."

"Thank you Sir, a very smart explanation. One has to be pragmatic, no good if one thinks the world is something which it is not. The economy is definitively the basis for all things. All wars were and are fought for economic reasons. Only a defensive war is righteous, any offensive war is simple aggression."
"This is too simplified, Sol. When thinking of war from a non-personal perspective, observing it as an analytic mind, one comes to different conclusions. For example, a smart leadership will always seek to fight a war against an enemy they can easily beat. If possible, you never fight a war on your home turf, unless it is unavoidable. You fight only limited wars in regular intervals, so your military is always a veteran one, there are always instructors who pass on the actual combat knowledge to the

new generations. What you do more frequently, is you think of the economy. Some smart leadership does not fight wars. They hire others to do the fighting for them.”

“What about the economy? What about economic growth?”

“The whole concept of eternal growth was conceived at a time when we had seven times less humans on the planet than we have now. One realizes soon enough that any domestic market can only consume as much of everything before they get too spoiled, then you need to invent ever more, often useless products and services to keep the people busy and content. You don’t get much new wealth out of a saturated market. You have to expand. You go to new markets. You go to places where people are hungry for products, services, and the experiences you can deliver. Though everyone is pursuing this mantra of endless growth, some people say that this is no longer feasible. A new concept, a new model for the economies of the world will have to be found, and until that happens, everyone is making the best he can out of the still existing model.”

“Mr. Max, a single person cannot cope with as much information that is needed even if such information is made available. A single person has the tendency to simplify, and to see the world as being black and white only.”

“You make a good point here. Think of this: most people take everything for granted. The more you give them, the more they want. Not everyone knows the difference because not many have lived it. I have noticed this in your essays; this is why we extended you the scholarship. Our interest lies with humans whose brains are capable of understanding the subtle differences. You have the potential for this. That is why we are talking to each other. Regarding the people as people, roughly at the same time when the Scottish economist wrote his masterpiece, and the founding fathers wrote the declaration of independence, another Scotsman wrote very interesting pieces about the likely cycles of societies with a solid remark about democracy. The gentleman was a lawyer, writer, and historian. He was very critical of democracies and for good reasons, too. Much of his work has been lost; thus, it is uncertain that the conclusions accredited to him are really what he said. Perhaps his surviving work inspired others who then created conclusions based on his work. Regardless of the true origin of the thought, the final product that appears from time to time is very interesting."

"Sir, what is the teaching that is accredited to this Scottish intellectual?"

"Simplified version tells that there are repeating cycles in history that portray the state of mind of the general public, which define the relationship between the people and their government. The nine different phases or cycles that repeat themselves are: bondage, spiritual faith, courage, liberty, abundance, selfishness, complacency, apathy, and dependence. What this means is that the general public starts as slaves. Then there is spiritual faith that life could be different. This is followed with actual courage to do what is needed to change the circumstances of life in order to achieve liberty. Happy people, who still remember that in the not-so-distant past life was less enjoyable, are quite productive. Such a society is characterized by abundance. Unfortunately for the people and the society in general, abundance leads to selfishness. At this point, one can witness that far too many people start to think about how to extract maximum gain from a functioning society. Too many people are asking for their rights, which are just the intent of the people to afford a higher standard of living at the cost of society. This leads to the society becoming weak and unjust. Those who are productive realize that they are the fools of the day. Then it gets quick, since complacency is followed by apathy. In the final phase comes dependency, because the only way to assure all these material rights, which more and more people are demanding, is to distribute and manage the wealth of the society by centralized means. The final phase, dependency, means that almost all people of the society are dependent upon the state for their survival. Sooner than later, the state cannot afford it and starts to downsize these material rights to some levels that are truly miserable. Eventually, a society that started as slaves also ends as slaves. Then the cycle begins again!"

"We did not learn about this, or if this gentleman was mentioned, I did not memorize it. If one looks at it as cycles then one can predict where a society is heading. Is it only related to democracies?"

"What is a democracy, Sol? Some of the most brutal regimes have this word as part of the official name of the state. Democracy is the rule of the masses. In today's world, anyone who controls the media is in control of the masses. Democracy can mean that a system is smart in making the masses believe that they, the people, are in charge, and, thus, the people go along with whatever reality they are served by those who actually call the shots. The mentioned nine cycles depend upon the definition of what a generation is. A generation is the time between being born and becoming a parent. Some places it can be only 15 years, most places it is about 25 years. Thus, the complete cycle could be about 200 years."

"Mr. Max, let us move to the present time. Now that the Communist model is bankrupt what comes next?"

"Bankruptcy is not the end of the world. Bankruptcy has a real purpose and can provide excellent long-term results. It is an opportunity for a fresh start. Lessons learned. A new start is made possible. It is tough though, but it can be positive. All systems go bust at some point. One develops an impression, a model world in which a model set of rules and behavior patterns are preferred. Some need the secret police to reinforce this model. It is the easy way of doing things. It is often better not to know the truth. All systems have a life span. Knowledgeable people and institutions have ways of making sound estimates concerning the life span of any system. There are mathematical formulas for this. Now that Communism went bankrupt, how about Capitalism going bust? Perhaps we may witness the emergence of new versions of past concepts. Repackaged, rebranded and then sold to the people. How about free market Socialism? Maybe there will be something called Productive Collectivism, or perhaps, Progressive Post-Modern Distributive ism… it can be anything. Communism may not be gone, but it is only temporarily suspended. You have to understand that Communism will have even greater appeal with the masses once the 'masses no longer have the benefits of it. There is no better system for the really wealthy than Communism. The population is under total control and nobody may even dare to question the demi-gods, the real rulers behind the scenes. The bottom line is, all of these "isms" are simply there to keep the society functioning. There have always been people who have more knowledge than others, people with more wealth and people with better skills. A society cannot function on the basis of chaos. If you have chaos, you have no society. Same time, chaos serves those who are organized. It is a mirage, a dream of a world and a society of truly equal people. People never were and never shall be equal, because this would understand that all people are clones, born on the same day, same place, brought up in identical social circumstances. Now that would be a boring world, would it not? Some people rule, others follow the rule. It's been like that ever since the beginning of mankind. It will be so for as long as there is a human species. It is the order of things in the human universe."

"The ancient Greeks analyzed this perfectly. Professor Wunderberg taught us that thousands of years ago, there were people who explained it all."

"The professor is a very smart man. People in general have an extremely short life span. You cannot organize and create anything of collective value in such a short life span. This is why the masses follow in the footsteps of some agendas prepared for them by their ancestors. The masses, especially if they are poorly educated or wrongly educated or not educated at all, have one general thing in common – impulsiveness. Their decision-making process is reasonably self-centered. A roof over the head, food in the stomach, and sex, those are the first-priority needs for most people. Decisions are made instantly, without thinking it over, without analysis of the total picture and likely consequences. Decisions are based on emotions, and emotions are understood as the only trustworthy platform upon which an individual builds his understanding of the world. The people tend to think of themselves as being smart, shrewd, informed, and knowledgeable. They can never be wrong about anything. If something goes wrong, you simply blame it on someone else. That has been so for ages, and it is not much different today. Different people grouped in different tribes, different tribes grouped in different nations, tend to have different experiences. So you get nations that are very good in almost anything they do, but no longer want to fight offensive wars because they had enough of it. Then you have nations that are willing to commit to foreign adventures, because they do not have the collective memory of what it means. This is why propaganda is so important. If you serve the people with sufficient, deliberate information, they will start to believe it. You can sell whatever to the masses, of course, with the difference of what these masses remember from their ancestors or even better, personal lives. It is important to understand human nature when one thinks about society. There is no, there was no, and there will hardly ever be a perfect system which regulates affairs.

Such need to be regulated since otherwise there is chaos."

"What about the society itself growing tired and losing the grip over daily affairs."

"Interestingly, also in 1776, a British historian published the first of a total of six volumes of his epic work that addresses the decline and fall of empires. Much of what he wrote then can be applied today."

"Yes Mr. Max, we studied it at the University, it was about the Roman Empire."

"Yes, the Roman Empire, both its western and eastern branches were the longest lasting empires in documented history. The general trend is that empires last shorter and shorter. At some point, the empire will have its golden age that usually lasts one or perhaps two generations. During the golden age, great achievements in science, arts, craftsmanship, and social engineering occur. After the golden age, comes the inevitable decline."

"You are a rare species Mr. Max. Most people I know of or heard of are obviously not as sophisticated as you are."

"You are young. You got lots of time to meet very different people. I am certain that in 20 years from now, you will know many different, yet special people. Certain types can be found in certain places. It depends on whether you are invited or not. The trouble is that the system works the way that establishments don't like to be picked. They like to pick other people. A lot of talent and qualitative minds are lost in the process of life, because they never had the chance to roll out their full potential. This is something I would like to see changed. There were some well-meant theoretical projects in the past decades that looked into this, but it is still science fiction."

"Yes Sir, there were many theoretical projects that never materialized."

"It is the people themselves who do not want to hear bad news and do not want to act upon them. Do not be misguided by the well-meaning intellectuals who dream about a world that could be. There are reasons why not everyone is privileged to certain type of information. There are reasons why decision makers have to observe things just as they are, not as someone would like them to be. The real responsibility also includes a good stomach to digest all the problems one learns about in due process of being in a position of power. The world is like a garden, unless you keep constant watch, various new plants will start to grow. Not necessarily did you want them to grow – you just did not pay attention; you had no time. Last but not least, a crisis first has to emerge before people start to deal with it. Preemptive action is not exactly a human trait."
"Do your clients consider preemptive action?"

"Some of our clients make preemptive action a part of their business. When you take the necessary time, put together some very bright minds, take into account historical precedents, grind and digest it all together, apply custom-made mathematics, and process it in super computers, then you can get a series of possible outcomes. This is our daily bread at the Institute. We do not predict the future. We provide a very educated best guess about any number of scenarios that might occur, and we serve these findings to the paying clients. These paying clients are responsible for hundreds of millions, billions, and even a trillion of something, say Dollar, Deutsch Mark, Yen, or whatever currency. Such people have to know what the possibilities are in order to control their own risk exposure. This is the world of real analysis and real computer simulations. Analysis of this sort, and simulations that provide insights in the possible outcomes, has been practiced throughout history. The better the technology got, the better the product became. In the 1960s, you had analysis and simulations of international relations, political processes, business- and marketing processes and outcomes, career counseling, dreams, education, disaster relief, and handling of natural catastrophes. The whole Cold War was thoroughly analyzed and computer simulated in the U.S. and the Soviet Union. The 1970s introduced similar models in the fields of human action, and the whole dynamics of the world got thoroughly analyzed and simulated. It is not that one does not know what is likely to come. It requires serious effort to provide such insights. It is expensive. Not everyone needs such information and even less people can pay for it. We cannot sell illusions to our clients. Our job is to differentiate between wishful thinking and the cruel reality. We cannot use ideals in the scope of our work!"

"Sir, I know that things seldom are as what they seem to be. Our beliefs are often someone else's programming and our illusions are even worse. It is better to come to terms with the truth than to wake up one morning in shock."

"Again, this might not be so. The majority of people will probably rather opt to live in some sort of a manufactured illusion and enjoy it while it lasts."

"Does the Institute research geo-politics?"

"Yes. We have a very accurate database which represents the world. It addresses many different issues, climate, food production, politics, balance of power, and economy; thousands of variables are taken into account. Most of our assignments are in the domain of providing risk exposure estimates, and we do a lot of product ideation, developing new products and services for our clients. We do not council our clients on geo-political issues but geo-politics is part of our computer simulations."

"You mentioned a definitional mission before I could become an employee of the Institute. What is the real purpose of the definitional mission if I may ask?"

"To have been someplace, to have seen it and lived it is different than theoretical knowledge and TV experience. The purpose of the definitional mission is for you to see, whether the reality that will be revealed to you, if it is something you can cope with. We had cases where potential candidates decided to choose a different life path in which they could live in their own reality, a reality they preferred. You got a great education but it is all theory. The work we do is not dangerous; it is not even thrilling. We have to be very realistic about every detail of our work. If we are not, we might serve our clients with a faulty product."

"I understand. You repeatedly emphasize realism."

"The basis of our work is to understand the world we live in. This is why we can provide expert and professional analysis of almost any topic that is of concern to our clients. Most of our assignments are in the domain of less interesting topics, but sometimes we receive challenging and creative assignments."

"If I may ask, how do we proceed from here? Now is August, when would the definitional mission be?"

"I am departing for Europe tomorrow. We would like to welcome you at the Institute in about two weeks from today. Plane, lodging, food, and a reasonable compensation for your time before and during the definitional mission are covered by the Institute. You will be introduced to the Institute's facilities; we will show you some of the things we do, some of the equipment we use, including the visual presentation tools. Then you would receive several mentors who will teach you how the process works, plus you will be expected to read about the history of the countries where the definitional mission will take you. You have to be prepared. Did you hear of the five P rule?"

"No Sir, I am not familiar with that rule."

"Memorize it. Proper Preparation Prevents Poor Performance. In order to maximize the learning benefits of the definitional mission, you first have to be properly prepared for it. In order to have a chance of understanding events in the field, you first need to learn about the backgrounds of the places you will visit. I don't want you to ask stupid questions when you're in the field. Only through such a process will you be able to distinguish between theory and practice. You will mature after you've gone through the definitional mission, I am sure of it."

"Do other members of the Institute go through their own definitional missions before receiving employment with the Institute?"

"Some do, not all of them. It depends what their assignment with the Institute is. Someone working on data processing needs no definitional missions, he needs specialist training. We would like you to develop into an analyst who can one day be trusted with the integration of various findings. This means we will invest in you. You would receive additional education in computer sciences, psychoanalysis, and economy. Because of the total-desired projection of what we would like to see develop out of you, we have to be sure that you want to do it. And in order for you to be sure, we have to expose you to the reality of things."

"This is a prudent strategy, Sir."

"It is a necessity. The Institute is in the business of providing educated council to the decision makers. We cannot afford to have brain-clouds in our own judgment. If you seek to be a young millionaire, then the work with us is not the right thing for you. If you seek political power, we are the wrong address. Please memorize this.”

“Yes Sir, I am getting the picture. Thank you.”

“Young man, I think we had some quality time. This is my business card. Call the office and they will arrange all the details, timing, air travel, and expense money for you. I expect to see you in Switzerland in two weeks.”

“A thousand thanks Mr. Max. I am most appreciative of your attention and offer.”

THE INSTITUTE

Zurich International Airport, September 1993.

Though having lived in Europe most of his life, Sol missed the
opportunity to visit Switzerland. The Swiss evolved and learned from the
times in which small chiefdoms fought against each other and learned the
benefits of being united, sharing both interests and responsibilities. The
Swiss orientation to be a neutral country enabled them to create a specific
economy and reach a very high standard of living in a setting, which, other
than the natural beauty of the Alps, gave very little economic incentive
when compared to many other countries. Sol boarded a cab at the airport
and enjoyed the sceneries until the cab reached the address of the Institute.
Sol took his suitcase and walked to the reception building. The Institute
positioned itself at the end of a small valley. It was a typical clean and
green village of the kind one finds in Switzerland, Bavaria, Austria, or the
northern parts of Italy. It reminded Sol of the cult TV series from the
1960s, except this village was not a prison for international spooks like the
TV village was. Sol was expected thus the procedure in the reception
building was swift. A young lady, dressed in casual Jeans, invited him to
take place in an electrical vehicle, similar to the type used on Golf terrains.
A quiet drive through the main street of the Institute's village where they
passed by typical Swiss houses, all looked very pleasant and welcoming.
As they stopped in front of one of the houses, the lady invited Sol to
unpack and get some rest before he would meet Mr. Max at the main
office building in one hour. She would pick him up. One hour later, Sol
found himself in front of a very specific piece of architecture: A perfect
hemisphere made of aluminum and glass. Upon entering the building all
looked like an episode from a sci-fi movie. Everywhere he looked, there
were trees and plants, a very green and pristine atmosphere, almost like a
botanical garden. The young lady brought him to an elevator and excused
herself. The glass elevator took Sol to the top of the building. As the
elevator door opened, the familiar face of Mr. Max welcomed him.

"Welcome Sol. I officially welcome you to the Institute. I hope your travel was fine."

"Sir, you said your ancestor built some houses for the employees, but I never thought to see a grown village, plus this hemisphere building with lots of green. It looks like a spaceship that is self-sufficient. I am amazed."

"I said that we put special emphasis on having our associates work in quality conditions. It is all about quality. If you have content people, then the product of their work will be of better quality. These are the principles we follow in everything we do. Architects considered that a setting with lots of trees and plants would provide the desired results. The housing areas are well maintained, but much of it was built in the 1930s. The working areas are state of the art. Here, let me show you the area plan of the Institute. On this map, you can see that the Village occupies almost 200 hectares of land. The Institute houses 80 associates and their dependents. This area here is the production area – the hemisphere building. Here our associates do their work, but many can also do their work from home. All of it is very handy and serves the objective of delivering prime quality product to our clients. The production area also has underground levels. These are predominantly for maintenance and utilities purposes, plus storage areas where much of the computer hardware and data storage is held. This area here is where our local grocery store is. Next to it is the kindergarten and closed playground for the children. We have our restaurant that serves two warm meals per day. We have a big gym, a 25 meter swimming pool, a bowling track, inside Squash terrains and so on. As you can observe, these green areas are our parks. There is a dedicated jogging path for those who like to run. And up there, what looks to be empty space, this is the pasture area. We have our own cows that live long and happy lives. A local family is employed to take care of the green, the pasture, and the cows. We have a small maintenance team and a small security detail on premises. There is a car pool for our employees and a stretched limousine for our clients. We have our own minibus that drives our children to school. We have our own legal department and all the corporate stuff one needs. In the next valley, westwards, some 20 kilometers from here is a small airfield which handles corporate jets. Everything is neat and well organized. Many clients like to come and stay for a week, which makes sense given the amount of data we often have to discuss. Why not make it comfortable for both the guests and our associates who have to present it? All in all, this is it. I will show you some of the working areas later."

Mr. Max's office was roundly shaped. Since the building had the design of a hemisphere, the office was on the very top. It had a 360 degree view of the village and the surrounding mountains. A magnificent view, many people would like to have such an office. Inside the office, Sol and Max sat down at a round table on very comfortable chairs.

"Let me introduce you to the way we do things here. Here is how an average assignment is handled. Each project gets its project manager. The project manager signs the eventual findings and as the art and science of project management go, the manager has to have the skills of combining and integrating the knowledge and experience of all members of the team. He or she has the biggest workload of all and has to study everything. Discipline of one's own ego is crucial since in order to work with people, who know more than oneself in particular fields of expertise, the manager has to be a true adult. The project manager has two assistants. These carry out all the internal correspondence, take care of the project checkpoints, and so on."

"Then we have the actual teams. Depending upon the project assignments, we create the teams accordingly. Many teams if needed. And here we rely on outside associates as well – people like Professor Wunderberg, for example. Some projects take several hundred minds to produce the expected end result. All the data and opinions are thoroughly checked before we have the final deliverable. When all of this is done, then and not before, we feed our visual presentation tools, which are the two globes you will see shortly. The project manager and the board of directors then look at the variety of visual presentations. Usually, we have some small fine tuning, ironing-out of the whole package, and then we deliver it to our clients. You see, it is a very labor intensive process. This is why our employees live in our village, so they need not lose time commuting to their workplace and back. When needed, people pull 36 hour shifts, sleep for 12 hours, then do 36 hour shifts again. There are many night hawks, some of our associates do not like to socialize, and we put no pressure on them. We have top quality health care, a decent retirement program, best of life insurance, and a range of other perks. The objective of our care is to have the minds of our associates focused on the job, not tormented by their own problems. Associates who choose to live outside of the village are free to do so at their own expense. Some live in the nearby villages, mostly because they married locally. We are constantly educating ourselves. We are firm believers that life should be a life of education. For this reason, we have many workshops, and the teachers and instructors come and stay with us for the duration of the sessions."

Sol had been trying to conceal his impression of the village and the Institute until now, but was not very convincing.

"Sir, I think I start to understand why people like to work for the Institute or commission the Institute's services."

Mr. Max tended to overhear this youthful comment, changing to more serious topics.

"All of this costs money of course. Our services do not come cheap. Our clients pay the asked prices knowing that they will get top quality for their money. All of this is only possible because we save money or help create money for our clients. Our clients are the big businesses, others cannot afford this. We also do charitable work. On occasion, we will provide our services free of charge to various institutions and organizations who are involved in anti-poverty, humanitarian, or ecological protection programs. You care for any refreshment, water, juice, coffee?"

"No, thank you Sir, I'm just fine the way it is."

"Then let us take a tour of the production area. Here is your chip card. It is your ID here at the Institute. Some areas are closed to outsiders; some areas are accessible only based on seniority or the assignment. I ask you to have this chip card with you when you leave your apartment."

As the gentlemen walked through the production area, the scenery was pretty much the same. Lots of space, lots of green, small ponds with exotic fishes and every now and then, clusters of desks filled with big screens, computers and cables, charts on the walls, people dressed casually, discussing, working and reading. The generation span was obvious: one could see people from their mid-20s to the wise age of probably 70 and perhaps even more years. Here and there, quiet jazz or classic music could be heard. In one of the underground levels, Mr. Max opened a secure door that opened by reading the palm of his hand.

"Sir, I have never seen so much computing power. I am impressed."

"This is our main cluster of computers. It is all parallel computing. We thought of buying Cray's when these were the supercomputers of the day. But since some of our clients come from the IT industry, we bartered our services for this. You have 256 cabinets here, and each cabinet has multiple processors. I don't know the computing power or the storage power, and I don't care about these numbers. Our IT manager tells me that we have more computing power than most of the airlines."

"Sir, I am a big fan of computing myself."

"Of course you are, you are the generation that got born into the age when computing power was made available to the general public. I told you that our intent, if we come to terms, is to provide you with more education, including computer sciences. Multidisciplinary minds are what we appreciate. A combination of political sciences, history, economy, psychoanalysis, and computing can create completely different results than a mind that understands only one thing."

"You got full redundancy on this system, Sir?"

"Yes. Like all big computing users, we have another system, exact match of this one, which is in one of the abandoned mines in the nearby mountains. That's the redundant center. It is well below earth's surface. Plus we have triple redundancy on our power supplies."

"Sir, it is almost like NORAD from the movies."

"Perhaps, with one big difference, we are not of importance to be the target of nuclear missiles. When you see our visual presentation tool, you'll think of NORAD from the movies differently. We are much, much more interesting."

Walking through the tunnel that connects the production facility with the leisure area, the gentlemen entered the restaurant.

"It is self-service. There is no a la carte food served, except when people have birthdays or we have special guests on premises. You have buffet choice."

The restaurant functioned in similar manners like the production area, kind of a creative chaos perhaps. People come and go, without any specific order or schedule. Sol was hungry, something that can happen after long haul flights, so he was quite zealous in repeated choices from the buffet.

"Great food Sir, compliments to the chef. You don't have food replicators here? I mean, it all looks like a spaceship."

"I have to laugh Sol; you really are the TV series generation. We do have a gentleman scientist who has very specific ears. He works on the computer modeling part of our job, but I don't think he comes from the planet Vulcan."

"The food is excellent, I am sorry, but the flight and time zones make me hungry."

"Eat young friend, everything you see here is free of charge. I would recommend you to try our milk. You don't get many chances to drink fresh milk these days."

"Sir, I like everything I see here. I am not yet sure that this is happening to me."

"We invited you and this is happening to you. If you are finished with the food, let us go to the movies. Today you will see something I am sure you have never seen in your life before. It takes a lot of computing power to do it."

Relaxed and fed, Sol followed Mr. Max in his walk to the production area. This time they took the surface path. Back in the main office building, the glass elevator took them underground. What opened in front of them was a classic amphitheater.

"Welcome to the Agora. Just like in ancient Greece, the purpose of this amphitheater is similar. This is where the visual presentation to our clients takes place. We can accommodate up to 100 people. Sometimes we use this area for community fun since it has excellent acoustics, being a real model of a real amphitheater. Let us take a seat in the first row. Everything in this area is voice controlled. We had voice control many years before others used it. It is not a very recent technology for your information."

"Now, this is where science fiction starts. Shut the lights!"

Except for the small orientation lights in the floor, the Agora was completely dark.

"Computer, prepare the standard globe simulation please."

A warm and pleasant voice, neither male nor female, responded.

"Standard globe simulation initiated. Please choose your scenario."

"Let's start with scenario one."

In the center of the podium, two identical electronic globes appeared. One could not say what diameter, but probably at least five meters each. Simultaneously, the globes rotated around their axis, like identical twins. The surface of the globes could not be identified by looking at it; it looked like a hologram, light blue in color. Then the computer voice started to narrate:

"Welcome to the globe simulation tool. The globe to your right represents the world as we know it. The globe to your left shows how it can be, how it could have been, or simply, it shows the contents of the analysis conducted by this Institute. Both globes are state of the art technology. They can both expand in diameter and you can zoom in on them. They may have additional functions from the ones just described. Please issue command for the start of the presentation."

"Sir, I did not know something like this exists."

"This technology was part of a major project some years ago. We opted to be paid in-kind for our services. We defined what we wanted and the industry provided us with the product. It is quite expensive. For your information, similar things will be commercially available and affordable in perhaps 20 years from now. Are you ready? Brace yourself, it's very impressive."

"I am ready Sir, let the voyage commence."

"Good. We will start with the most vivid sample case: The spread of civilization from 3000 B.C. till 1990 A.D. In a minute, the right globe will show how the effects of mankind's influence on the habitat, urbanization of the planet, and nature. Red flashes represent wars. In this version of the simulation, the left globe shows how the world would have developed if mankind had intelligently used acquired knowledge from past mistakes and developments. We used a hypothetical model in which by the year 0, mankind learned from its mistakes and all further development was made in sustainable ways, including much less warfare and a socio-political system of governance that is balanced, meaning a world where poverty is a thing of the past. Every 100 years, the simulation stops and you will see the estimated number of humans expressed in numbers. Computer, please start scenario one!"

For the next hour Sol was left speechless. Both globes looked very similar till the year 0, but then the differences became dramatically evident. The simulation stopped in the year 1990, the right globe representing the world as it currently was: Polluted, deforested, and with dozens of red flashes (wars). The left globe, representing the world as it could have been had the humans evolved from their self-centered, selfish and aggressive patterns of behavior, looked dramatically different. It resembled paradise to Sol.

"Sir, I am stunned. Especially the development of the population: 1 billion people on the planet by around the year 1800, 2 billion people by 1930, 3 billion people by 1960 and so on. And all these wars, seeing it graphically, I am amazed with the constant presence of organized slaughter throughout history."

"Yes young man, humans are the worst of all animals. The purpose of the globes is to provide a global view at things. Our findings are presented in the form of documents, charts, and computer simulations that are viewed on normal computer monitors. The globes help acquire a global outlook. Astronauts reported that the world looks very different from the orbit, and the globes try to mimic that.

If you are ready we can go to the next scenario, this one covers the time from the year 1900 till 2100 and addresses climate change. We do not do climate modeling ourselves, we borrow the results from the various research institutes around the planet. What you will see is the medium value, meaning, the medium forecast from more than two dozen studies and simulations about the climate and how humans affect it. The right globe represents the known situation and continues into the future with the same values, meaning pollution and population levels as we have them by 1990. The left globe will start rotating by 1990 and takes into account population growth and the possible industrialization trends in the countries of the world that have not yet embarked on full industrialization. Computer, please start scenario two!"

The next hour of presentation left Sol speechless, again. This time the presentation focused on the effects of pollution and degradation of the biosphere.

"Sir, this is really terrible. Significant regions of the planet become uninhabitable. Do the decision-makers know about this?"

"Yes, some do. Nobody really knows for sure how this will play out but it is certain that mankind will not come to any reasonable agreements. Of course, we have seriously polluted our planet but climate change was part of Earth's history before there were industrial civilizations, or at least those we know of. Our sun has immense influence on everything that is happening on Earth. There is absolutely nothing that mankind can do about the sun. Some researchers say that the 21st century will be the century of Mother Nature's reaction to the human species. The planet adapts, the planet lives on, and the complex climatic conditions change.

Let us now take a look at a commercial topic. The right globe represents the spread of whatever product without aggressive propaganda, or advertisements, in a world that has functioning national borders and protective commercial barriers. The left globe represents a world without national borders, no commercial barriers, and very aggressive propaganda or aggressive advertisements. The time span is 10 years. It starts in 1990 and ends in 2000. Computer, please start scenario three!"

The simulation has shown that in a world with functioning national interests, the penetration level of the markets is low. The world without protectionist measures allowed any product to dominate much of the world markets in less than 10 years.

"So, this is what globalization is all about in visual terms?"

"Sol, globalization is nothing new. Perhaps the first documented globalization occurred from China, and was epitomized through the Silk trade routes. In that period China's trade influenced almost all of Asia, the Middle East, and even Europe. This was a thousand years ago. Then you had the colonization period which introduced European culture to distant countries and continents – this was also a globalization. A political idea, diseases, religious concepts, everything that can spread around causes a globalization moment. What is common with all of the past and current globalization moments is that it favors certain groups of people. If the globalization was commercial in nature, then it favored traders, speculators, freight forwarders, and bankers. If it was religious in nature, it would favor the clergy. Let us look at this current globalization hype. The next situation looks at the impact the current globalization has on the middle classes of the industrial world. The right globe represents an unchanged world from 1990 till 2020. The left globe represents the world during the same period which is subject to accelerated globalization. Blue color represents territories that have 40% or more of middle class citizens, while the red color represents territories with huge seas of poverty and a tiny fraction of extremely wealthy people. Please note that the main guarantee for a society to thrive and be at peace is the existence of a significant middle class. Societies where poverty is predominant are always run by a dictatorship. Computer, please start scenario four!"

The two globes started to rotate. The right globe represented the world as it was known by 1990. All the Western democracies had a significant percentage of middle class citizens and were colored in blue. The third world countries and the former communist bloc countries were colored in red. When the simulation stopped in 2020, the left globe portrayed a dramatically different world. The third world countries did not reach the blue color, and most of the Western democracies had lost their blue color. By 2020, the vast majority of countries would be completely absent of a functioning middle class.

"Sir, this means that by 2020, the world is in danger to lose its middle class and become a suitable ground for the rise of more dictatorships!"

"Young man, the transfer of jobs from the first to the third world has significant impact. This new round of globalization will result in a world with almost no middle class. National governments, which did not prevent the demise of their competitive economic powers, will become failed states or dictatorships."

"Will this work?"

"That remains to be seen. It depends upon many factors, but right now, globalization is winning."

"How will this globalization influence the future of this Institute?"

"The world is changing all the time. Knowledge is not reserved to a particular group of people. People, regardless of race and religion, are capable of learning. This Institute is not afraid of any competition. We like competition because it keeps us awake. If someone wants to offer the same expertise and services as we do, someone needs to invest huge amounts of money, plus spend at least 20 to 30 years of hard work to even come close to the level we are now. We constantly learn and improve our methods. The world is changing, people learn and become wiser.
Let us go to the next sample simulation. This one is about nuclear war. In this simulation, the right globe shows a small nuclear exchange of perhaps 50 Hiroshima-sized tactical warheads being used. The left globe shows a full nuclear exchange involving all nuclear weapons available to the human race after the end of the Cold War. Please note that by 1993 there

is much less nuclear weapons available to humanity than 20 years ago. Computer, please start scenario five!"

The globes presented a grim outcome. Contrary to the simulations of a full nuclear exchange at the height of the Cold War, the simulations have shown that in the worst case, perhaps one third of the world population would die and the remaining two thirds would survive. Their reality upon surviving the nuclear war would be hard. There would be serious food shortages and famine. Much of the civilizational amenities such as clean running water, electricity, transportation, health care and education would be seriously disrupted. A significant portion of the survivors would be seriously ill, not only due to radiation but due to the spread of all sorts of viruses and diseases. After a nuclear war, the populations of the world could only survive in some organized manner if martial law was introduced. Apart from a select few, the reality in a post-nuclear war would be very grim, but the coming generations, who know nothing of the past, would believe that it is the way things should be.

"We are truly lucky that we avoided any of these two scenarios. How many nuclear detonations did we see since the Trinity event in the New Mexico desert?"

"By now, there have been a bit more than 2,000 nuclear detonations that we know of. Apart from the two bombs dropped on Japan in 1945, more than 2,000 nuclear tests were carried out in the atmosphere, under the earth's surface, under water, and over land and sea of course. But they never detonated all at the same time, and except for the two in Japan, none were detonated over urban areas; thus, there were no huge quantities of dust and debris. The cumulative effect of all these tests is actually not really known. In any case, the nuclear weapons are the curse of humanity. I think you have seen enough, shall we go?"

"Thank you for these presentations. If I may ask, how many scenarios, or presentations does the Institute have?"

"We have several hundreds of different simulations. What you have seen are presentations. They are just for showing what our computing power can do."

How beautiful the world and how cursed mankind is were Sol's thoughts as he was leaving the Agora.

The following months, Sol prepared for his definitional mission that would start in February of 1994. In addition to extensively reading of history of the target countries, Sol also engaged in crash language courses that would help him when in the field. The wise sages, as the Institute called them – reputable and seasoned ladies and gentleman who were tasked with political analysis – devoted some of their time to Sol. Learning about the world affairs, Sol was frequently thinking about the time at Georgetown University. In his free time, Sol was enjoying the scenery, taking long walks in the foothills of the Alps. The views were magnificent, nature was beautiful, and he even learned how to milk cows. New Year's eve came with a nice celebration at the Institute. Small fireworks were reflecting in the glass hemisphere of the Institute's building; it all looked like a spaceship that had landed on Earth. One month later, the wise sages agreed that Sol was ready for his definitional mission. There was one final briefing ahead of him, and Mr. Max addressed him quite seriously:

"The wise sages tell me that you are as ready as a man of your age can be."

"Yes Sir, I am ready. The wise sages invested lot of their time and attention to make me understand the realities of the world. My emphasis should be to try to understand the various economic aspects of a country undergoing a transition between different economical models, and I am to focus on issues of what war really means."

"Sol, you will see and hear things that are real. A different reality will open up to your senses. Most of what you will hear and see is not pleasant.

It is important that you remember some basic rules. These rules will help you in most of the situations ahead of you. Let us start with the thought of being a good guest. When you go to foreign places, you follow their rules. If you are not welcomed as a guest, you leave. In general, depending upon your acts and behavior, people will extend you a mirror image. If you're impolite you get the same, if you are a diplomat you will receive similar attitudes. Except for places that are out of control and with people who are absolutely radicalized, a guest who knows how to behave seldom has any trouble."

"I will memorize this. Sounds like a proper strategy."

"Good. Here is then the rule about nationalism. I am certain that the Maker will not ask me whether I was an American, Chinese, French, German, Japanese, Korean, Navajo, Norwegian, Russian, Swiss, or an alien from outer space. The Maker will ask me what sort of a person I have been. Throughout history, it was the means of organized violence that made others agree with the order of things imposed on them. All civilizations did it this way. Avoid talks about the West or the East, North and South. Locals tend to forget that their society pillaged someone in the not so distant past. There is almost no nation that did not, at some point in history, attack their neighbors. Most people tend to forget this. Societies also change. The leaderships make a society aggressive or not. It is absolutely wrong to put blame on the children or grandchildren for the actions or inactions of their ancestors. A nation that committed atrocities, 50 or more years ago, has changed if the regime has changed. Avoid any discussions about ethnicity and religion. Focus on the actual events, do not comment them, watch and learn. Be a compassionate person. Last but not least, always follow our code of conduct. Do you remember what our code of conduct is?"

"Yes Sir, the Institute's code of conduct is as follows:

-       No politics. We do no not discuss politics when in the field.

-        No arrogance. Be a diplomat, be compassionate, and use empathy at all times. The person in front of you is the most important person in your life at that particular moment."

"Sol, you're prepared for the definitional mission. Your plane departs tomorrow from Zurich. You have all the things you need, credentials, plastic cards, money, the proper clothing, and you are mentally prepared. In three months from now, you will be a very different person. You will be more mature. If there are any troubles, there is always someone around who will pick up the phone. In Moscow, you will experience what life in a civilized society undergoing extremely harsh times looks like. Additionally, because the Soviet empire collapsed, it is possible that you hear from seasoned masters of specific human affairs, how the world really functions. You cannot get such input in Europe or the U.S. except if you are a chosen one. Use this opportunity and listen carefully. Zagreb, the capitol of Croatia, is the best logistical place for you to experience war and stay unharmed. Most of the current fighting goes on in Bosnia; you will see for yourself how ugly war is. Upon returning to Zagreb, you can learn a few things from a friend of mine. He is a former top level international diplomat who now works for the United Nations. Listen to him carefully as well."

"Thank you Sir, see you in three months!"

CHAPTER 2: DIFFERENT REALITIES

(1994)

This world is a comedy to those that think, a tragedy to those that feel.

Horace Walpole 

THE REVELATION

Sol had an early morning start. He had two flights to make, starting from Zurich with a short stop-over in Frankfurt am Main. His mind was wide open. Leaving the familiar world of Western Europe behind him, looking at the runway, Sol thought about all the people before him who embarked on a voyage into the unknown.

February 2, 1994, Moscow, Russia

SVO, as the abbreviation goes for one of Moscow's airports, did look differently than most airports Sol had visited before. An elderly man held a big sign with the letters "Institute," and Sol knew that this is his mentor for the time he will be in Russia. Half an hour later, both men were busy cleaning frost from the windshield of the car from the inside. The mentor was a cheerful person and addressed Sol accordingly.

"Mr. Max is a great friend of mine. We met for the first time more than 20 years ago in Rome. Those were great times. We had participated in the scientific simulations that modeled the possible future of the planet. Of course, today is different. Mr. Max runs the Institute and has some of the best computing power at his disposal. I am trying to do my work on some old personal computers. Nevertheless we are still in the same business, trying to see what the future has to offer. I've been told that you are the potential fresh blood of the Institute and I am to help you mature and become wiser in an accelerated way. They say that you should learn about transitional economies while in Russia. They also tell me that you should learn about what it means when an Empire implodes. There is no better place to learn about this than in Moscow, I assure you. Call me Ivan, no need for formalities. I have many scientific titles but that's of no importance to me."

Sol was still struggling with the inner side of the windshield. Something was not working properly with the car's heating and ventilation.

"Thank you Sir, I mean, thank you Ivan. It is really cold outside, and the windshield is kind of frozen too."

"You'll get used to the cold, don't worry. Stalin used to say that his best generals are January and February. At these temperatures, simple machines, simple vehicles function best. This is an old four wheel drive, the ideal vehicle for Russia. The heating will be fully on in a couple of minutes, don't worry; the windshield will be fine, too. I guess you are hungry, yes?"

"I could use a nice dinner. What's the plan, do we go to my hotel?"

"We go to my place. It is time for you to meet a typical Russian family. My wife has prepared a special meal for you. No hotel as Mr. Max explicitly asked me to provide you with a typical housing solution; otherwise you may not understand the transitional economy at all."

"Understand, so no hotel, a rented apartment perhaps?"

"Of a sort yes, rented in any case, yes. I live in a typical socialist high rise. Many Russians live in apartments with different families in single rooms while sharing the kitchen and bathroom. I thought such a scenario might be a little too harsh for you. So I asked a neighbor of mine, her family is out of town for the time being, whether she is willing to accommodate a young scholar who wants to learn more about Russia, and she agreed. You'll have a nice room with heating at her place. She lives across the street from me, so you'll be near to my place too."

"Great, I mean, a heated room sounds great. What do I pay for the room?"

"You pay nothing. Save your money. The lady is in her 80s so you will help her out, go to the market and bring stuff she needs. Trust me – it will do wonders for you."
"I am certain it will."

Sol's first evening in the world, which he had read a lot about and extensively studied during his time at Georgetown, was a revelation of its own. The dinner at Ivan's home was magnificent. People he never met before extended him such hospitality and warmth that he could not believe that they are complete strangers. Ivan's wife was a retired opera singer, while his two daughters were studying music. After the dinner, there was a small concert in the honor of the young guest who had just arrived from Western Europe. It would be well past midnight, when Sol returned to his new home (room). The few hundred meters, he had to walk from one high rise to the other, seemed like an arctic adventure tale. The room was quite small but it was warm. His landlady was already asleep but she did leave a note in Cyrillic on the kitchen table, obviously these were the things Sol would need to buy in the local store.

In the morning, Sol met his landlady as she prepared him a modest breakfast and they exchanged some basic Russian words Sol had learned during his preparation time in the past couple of months. When words are not enough, people use sign language. Sol understood that he should go shopping. The Cyrillic was not really understandable to him, and he thought to simply buy everything a household needs. Dressed for cold weather, Sol started to explore the area around the high rise buildings, searching for a currency exchange office and a grocery store. After a while, he realized that the local grocery store had just a limited choice of supplies, and he could not find any place to exchange his Swiss Francs. He had to improvise, so he chose to try his luck and go downtown Moscow. A cab driver can be a person's best friend when exploring a new city, especially a new country. Sol found a group of cab drivers doing some basic maintenance of their old vehicles. He got lucky: one of them could speak a bit of English and a bit of German. Sol explained what he wanted, and the cab driver explained him that this will not be as easy as he thought, perhaps they would need a half a day to complete the errands. They first found a place to exchange currency. The cab driver advised him not to exchange too much money due to inflation. The cab driver gave him first hand explanations about the shortage economy, especially in the years before the fall of the Berlin Wall. Even worse was the time of the first reforms in the early 1990s. The stores would be almost empty; people would wait for hours to simply buy anything. Then they would barter products on the streets. The local currency became literary worthless in a matter of weeks as the prices rose by 500, 600, and even more percent. People's life savings suddenly became worthless. It had been extraordinary hard for the population. The situation is, nowadays, much better, especially if one has hard currency. Down-town Moscow, Sol found excellently supplied stores and recognized products he used to buy in Western Europe and the U.S. After several hours of driving and visiting several stores, Sol returned to his landlady with more than 40 kilograms of food products, detergents, wine, and cigarettes. The landlady could not believe her eyes, and Sol started to understand that the population not only went through extreme hardships but continued to live in limited, austerity conditions. Then Ivan arrived, and the two men sat at the kitchen table to exchange thoughts.

"Ivan, I had a real adventure today. How can people survive in such conditions of scarcity? The differences between the rich and poor are staggering. How do ordinary people live in such conditions?"

"Sol, this is the reality. In the old times, money was never abundant, and many consumer items were subsidized, same as utilities are even today. People had a job, often it was miserably paid so they were not very productive. Housing was free of charge, and public transportation was free or very cheap. All in all, we had the basics we needed and focused more on personal relationships than we would focus on money and consumerism. It was a centrally planned economy and the masses were not used to any form of a free market society. When the changes came, there were no recipes, no actual precedents. As the reforms came, state-owned-property became available for privatization. And since the members of the Communist administration, the so-called apparatchiks, managed everything, the changes gave these people not only the best positions but also the funds to privatize. In the old times, state property was subject to theft. As the free market reforms came, it became normal to increase this

53

practice. In the first years, after the fall of the Soviet Union, whole branches of the industry were sold to private investors for sometimes even less than 5% of the real market value. The people were completely unprepared for the changes. When the voucher privatization came, they were already so low on any money that they simply sold their vouchers to shrewd middleman who worked for organized groups who would, for very little money, become owners of factories and natural resources. At the same time, one could see lots of international businessman who recognized the opportunity and provided additional capital to the locals involved in privatization. Some young U.S. economists arrived to help out the government in the reforms, but they applied theories that were never before tested at such scale like in Russia. Theories that provided results in small, agricultural Latin American countries were not the proper theories for a huge collapsing economy which was predominantly industrialized, like the Soviet Union was. A combination of reforms, intensive battle for power between the various Russian factions, and the naivety of the general population resulted in a dramatically changed society as we see it now."

"Ivan, that's like the old saying; the road to hell is paved with the best of intentions."

"Yes young man, it is the theft of the century. From a society that did not provide many consumer choices, at all, but knew how to provide basic housing, some employment, basic food, and medical services for everyone, we moved into the feudal past of Russia. The total collapse of the economy, the implosion of the society, hunger, fear, panic, despair, all led to the rise of organized crime. Combinations of politicians, ex-military and secret service people, merciless capitalists, and sufficient quantities of international businesses do what they please in this country. The people are hopeless; the life expectancy of males has dropped to 55 years only, much of it has to do with rampant alcoholism.
It is easy to define transitional economies, but what is actually happening is that the minds of the people are in transition as well. Rule of law collapsed. Luckily, many of the institutions created during the Soviet times, still exist and, thus, the people have, at least, some services

provided to them at low or no cost at all. The system of free housing meant that most people have, at least, a place to live, which is important. One can survive and starve for long times if one has at least some home. Had this been a system of housing where most property is burdened with mortgages, the situation would be even worse since huge numbers of people would become homeless. Once a person is homeless, the situation becomes hopeless."

"Ivan, I am depressed, though I will never truly understand it. I am here to learn. I have a decent budget and in a few months, I will be back in the West where a good job awaits me. Guess I would have to live this life of scarcity to really understand it."

"Mr. Max is a wise person. He told me that it is essential for your future development and role at the Institute that you become aware of the different realities of this world. Youthful idealism is great, but it is also fatal. He told me that you have great talent for analytic work and the Institute would like to invest in your further education as well. Use the next weeks to learn more about this reality and at the end of your Moscow experience, you will meet very knowledgeable people who may be of help for your perception of the world around us."

And so it was, Sol gradually immersed into the day to day life of ordinary Russians. In the coming weeks, he lived a life of an ordinary citizen of Moscow. He enjoyed in quality theatrical and musical plays that remained available to the public from the days of the Soviet Union. He mingled with people, learned about the culture, and more than anything, he learned how to have a rich social life without the usually required financial assets that go with it. At the very end of his Russian experience, his local mentor arranged for three more meetings. One with an esteemed Russian political scientist, one with a reputable economist, and last but not least, Sol would meet a high ranking manager of a weapons manufacturing company, a part of the dwindling, but still massive, military industrial complex that was an integral part of the Soviet Union, just as it was, and is, the case in some other countries.

A POLITICAL SCIETIST'S VIEW

"After the Second World War from the perspective of nations, the only true winners were the Americans. They fought no war on their home turf, had comparably low casualties and managed to get out of the economic depression through the immense production of military products and supplies. They turned out to be a benevolent hegemonic power that understood that profit comes from trade. This is what Pax Americana is all about – cheap oil, U.S. dollar as the global reserve currency, and the U.S. Navy in control of the sea trade lanes. Geostrategic positioning is an activity that stretches for centuries. Today one needs an enemy in order to build up own capabilities for tomorrow. Much of everything is a ruse. Let us focus on the past decades and the present. America has chosen to embark on the path of a permanent war economy. The Soviet Union pursued a similar path, but never possessed the economical means for a protracted arms race. The combination of bureaucratic inertia and corruption coupled with huge military spending literally bankrupted the economy. Of course, the image of a powerful enemy helped both leaderships assure allegiance of their populations. Important is to understand why some insist on the democratization of the world. The casual observer may think that this is because of real concern for the benefits of the people. This is where propaganda serves as a tool. A naive person may think that because 1 out of 500 people is a millionaire actually represents good odds to become wealthy yourself. A wise person knows that this ratio actually means that 1 out of 500 people gets born into a wealthy family. One of the great American scholars has put this democracy drive in its right context – the purpose of global democratization is to introduce a simplified version of democracy. The masses of people should be allowed to vote but the wealth distribution does not change. Even the creation of new wealth is not desired since it could upset things. Such a democracy exclusively serves the interests of money. Why? Because in such a democratic world, it is simple and cheap to influence events by means of non-governmental organizations, or simply put, activists. If the leadership of such a democracy suddenly has some independent ideas one simply instigates more or less peaceful revolt, using activists that are allowed in a democratic system. The local powers-that-be learn soon that unless they fall back into the line prescribed, they might not get re-elected. This is much cheaper than covert operations or military invasion. They have been quite successful in what they are doing. Though there were huge differences between the Soviet Union and the United States, there were also striking similarities. Both were post-WWII military-oriented industrial empires that embarked on the path of economic and technological growth. Both intimidated the whole planet through means of overt and covert actions, above all with the massive nuclear arsenals that could destroy all mankind within a few hours. Both built huge bureaucratic systems that are incapable of any reforms. Both were engaged in an ideological propaganda war and meddled with the internal affairs of all other nations. Perhaps the biggest similarity is that both empires brainwashed their population to believe that the world cannot function without them. This produces imperial aspirations and lack of realistic views of the problems of the world. All of this costs a lot of money, the Soviet Union went bankrupt but what is left, is the core power behind it, Russia. Time will show whether the U.S. will go bankrupt and how it will cope with bankruptcy. Personally, I do not think that the U.S. will ever go bankrupt because they have the ability to print money which is accepted by anyone. The problem with big military industrial complexes and the accompanying gigantic bureaucracies is that they have no interest in changing their missions. For six thousand years, the common solution to anything is to wage wars!"

Sol quietly listened to the wise analysis of a seasoned master of political sciences. Then he asked the big question;

"In your opinion Sir, what will be the predominant trend in the coming years?"

The seasoned political scientist replied with a big smile: "The re-emergence of national states of course, what else? The privileged classes, throughout the world, had enough of the two empires telling them what to do. Think of it in simple ways – two empires mean that only people from their ranks get to enjoy the real power perks. This world has perhaps 4,000 nations, and if privileged classes get organized in only 200 sovereign states, it still means that 200 privileged groups will have the opportunity to enjoy the advantages of being a president, an ambassador, a chief of armed forces, governor of the national bank, and so on. Most of them will not hold any global power, but that's irrelevant. They will yield their power over the populations they rule, and squeeze the poor in order to acquire their own wealth.

We had a trend of centralization that brought about huge empires that always bring with them a very privileged class of bureaucrats that manage everything. Now this trend is being reversed, and we will see the rise of nationalism which will guarantee the rise of many smaller privileged classes of bureaucrats. It is human nature, a huge percentage of people wish to enjoy the privileges that come from the positions of political power. Let me read you a quote from one of the world's great scholars, i.e. Thomas Jefferson in his Notes of Virginia, 1784:

'Mankind soon learns to make interested use of every right and power they possess or may assume. The public money and public liberty, intended to have been deposited with three branches of magistracy but found inadvertently to be in the hands of one only, will soon be discovered to be sources of wealth and dominion to those who hold them; distinguished, too, by this tempting circumstance; that they are the instrument as well as the object of acquisition.'

Jefferson identified it correctly young man. It has nothing to do with politics, religion, ideology, or whatever. It has everything to do with human nature."

Sol did not expect a reputable Russian to quote Thomas Jefferson, one of the founding fathers. More and more Sol understood what the wise sages at the Institute were telling him. The human nature is the cause of most trouble that the world faces. All events unfold in accord with the nature of decision-making.

The time rushed by, and Sol asked the political scientist another question:

"Since the prevailing trend will be the re-emergence of nationalism, are there any other options or trends to expect?"

"Yes, there are always opposing forces. One should not forget the one planet, one people, and one government agenda. The proponents of this worldview will do what they can to pursue this agenda just as they did in the past. In principle, the one planet and one people idea has lots of appeal and makes lots of sense. After all, we are one species. The issue is that the problems of the world are diverse and complex. It is easy to imagine and think of some great solution, sitting behind a comfortable desk in some air-conditioned office. It is a completely different thing when one tries to impose his viewpoint and agendas upon the diverse cultures around the planet. As a matter of fact, there are many variables that may be deceptive to the casual observer. A newly awaken national leadership that publicly pursues a national agenda may indeed be serving the one planet, one people, and one government agenda. The people in power outwardly give people what they want to see and hear, yet pursuing completely different objectives. Let us not forget that these opposing forces and interest groups live and work through the ages, and the true facts are known to a just a few. I am certainly not among those few who really know what the plan is."

AN ECONOMIST'S OPINION

"Let us focus on the situation immediately after the Second World War. The winners introduced a New World Order which regulated who does what. Most of Europe was completely devastated. The division of Europe between the Americans and Russians meant that two different economical models would influence the fate of these territories. The American model was more appealing, but it also had little other choice if the masses wanted stability. Western Europe always enjoyed a much higher standard of life than Eastern Europe. You could not give people much less than they remembered. The people got used to violence; thus, one could not introduce more violence in order to control the population. The alternative choice was to create the Western welfare state. It was a long-term strategy, and it worked well. It is mercantilism, opportunism, and one should not blame those who made profits out of the stupidity of European countries that engaged in two suicidal bloodsheds. The people of Western Europe also profited. Eastern Europe was always the European third world, and whatever natural resources and human labor could be found there, it was cheap. Russia itself was completely ruined, devastated as a consequence of the epic battles on the Eastern Front. There was neither the capital available, nor was there this entrepreneurial talent one finds in the West.

The emphasis was to provide the masses of people with the basics – a roof over their heads, basic utility, social services, food and work. And it worked, once Eastern Europe was no longer the third world of Western Europe, health care improved and educational opportunities improved multifold. A poor person coming from a remote village could become a highly educated and respected scientist, for free. A person in need of health services would get them for free. These are civilizational advances one cannot overlook. The other thing is that the planned economy and the Russian rule over its Eastern European satellites collapsed, because it was not self-sustainable in the long run. Right now, all the former communist countries are a huge pool of cheap labor and Russia is especially eyed because it does have immense natural resources. As a conclusion, our economic model failed first, this does not automatically mean that the current Western economic model is victorious. We are all capitalists now and as such, we will see a diversification of capitalism just as it happens with democracy. There is a Western European capitalist model just as there is a Western European model of democracy. There is an American capitalist model and an American model of democracy. There will be a Russian capitalist model and a Russian model of democracy. Nominally, the names that define a system may be the same, but there will be many differences as to how the system works in accord with historical and cultural specifics of a region."

"Sir, you view the future to be one of prevailing democracy and capitalism. Much of the world does not know about democracy, and there are some doubts about capitalism as such. Will capitalism develop in a humane fashion, or will it develop as described in some books originating in the 19th century?"

"Sol, you make a point here. In a monetary world, everything revolves around the question of money. We do not know for sure what is coming next. Optimistic people tend to believe that our future is bright and that advances in technology will bring a better tomorrow for everyone. Pessimistic people tend to believe that the future will be a dramatic increase of exploitation of everything, including the human resource. Nowadays, people are considered to be just another resource."

Sol could not overlook the fact that politics and economy are, of course, interconnected. The role of the Second World War was also very evident. World Wars introduce a new order of things practiced around the world. A nuclear world war would change the world even more profoundly.

A WEAPONS MANUFACTURER'S VIEW

"War was always the centerpiece of any society's capability to do something in an organized fashion. It has many useful roles which the general public does not recognize. First of all, to maintain any army requires a fixed percentage of the gross domestic product being projected into defense spending. This is important because one has, at least, some secure areas of governmental spending that cannot be disputed and are not subject to sudden market condition changes or speculations. Any war machine requires manpower, equipment and supplies. Therefore, it creates many assured jobs, which is also a stabilizing factor in any organized society. It also serves as a catalyst within the society. All societies face the problems of young males who do not know what to do with their lives and some think that they can bully around. You take such males into the military or police. You give them a meaning, provide them with harsh discipline and you got rid of the potential problems. In times of natural disasters, one can mobilize the military to provide aid and assistance. Military structures also provide additional authority throughout the society.

A military industrial complex can provide useful technological spin-offs that benefit the civilians. Last but not least, military power is hard power that prevents others from imposing their will over your society. Soft power, the power of bribes and cultural appeal may be more efficient in our times, but you still need hard power to survive. War and war machines have had and remain to have crucial functions in most societies."

"I understand Sir. You mentioned the draft when talking about young males. What about professional armies? How does one compare professional and conscript armies?"

"Conscript or civilian soldier armies tend to be less efficient. It depends upon the society and its economy. You need wealth to afford a dedicated professional army. Most have to rely on a huge pool of potential conscripts. In the Second World War, the Soviet Union mobilized immense quantities of people who were often sent to battle without sufficient weapons. It resulted in catastrophic losses, but it worked. In a democratic society, conscription armies cannot be sent to far away territories to fight any type of war. If you take a professional soldier; it is his work, his daily bread to fight a war if needed. If you take a civilian and mobilize him, he may perform well in defending his home turf but will always have second doubts about the whole affair and will look to get back home to his own life and family."

"How does a scenario of a professional army invading a country defended by a conscript army play out?"

"A professional army can surely win on the battlefield, especially if it is better equipped, if it has better weapon systems, and, above all, better training. History has shown that no invader really won in the long term by military means only. One needs huge quantities of own military personal to occupy even a small country. One has to create a local puppet regime with local police forces that are, at least, appearing to be loyal to the invader. In reality, one cannot really solve anything by military means only. Military might is best used for defending one's own interest against a foreign invader. A conscript army defending their country might dissolve on the battlefield, but it will use its basic military skills to stage a long guerilla war. If the people are really against an invader, the invader will always lose in the end, be they a professional army or not. This is why in recent history conquering territories is done by more subtle means."

"What would these subtle means be?"

"Bribing the privileged class of a foreign country to do what you tell them to do was always the most efficient and cheapest way. Instigating revolt, supporting the opposition by means of money and information is also not expensive. The best, of course, is to have the people, who you want to subdue to your rule, ask for you and love you. This is done by cultural means and by propagation of consumer products. This is the most efficient way because it directly subdues the conscious will of the target population. The real wizards can subdue other segments of the population by making them believe that they will have a much better life if they adopt whatever laws, cultural practices, and habits. Being in charge of the total finances of some other nation is also a great way of being in charge without having to resort to military means. If you are facing significant difficulties in the homeland, problems that basically affect your own ability to rule over your own people, then you manufacture a war. Your locals cannot complain because even if they do, they are traitors who endanger the strategic interests of national security. There is no business like war business!"

"I always thought this saying refers to show business?"

"Show business is laughable in comparison to war business, regardless whether it is war or peace time. Let me explain it to you. As I mentioned before, any military system is above all a huge and complex set of manpower, equipment, facilities, and supplies. This requires a lot of administration which means one can employ a lot of politically suitable and preferred people, like your own relatives. The actual productivity is in many cases close to nothing. First of all, you have all these salaries being paid for jobs that otherwise would not exist. All the equipment has to be manufactured. This again means more workplaces and profits, all of which are hard to account for. Who can really say, whether the true cost of manufacturing a main battle tank is one or ten millions of something? The equipment that is defined as military grade is an endless opportunity for over-pricing. Whatever you deliver to the military requires maintenance. Even if equipment is kept in storage, which is often the case, it will still require regular maintenance, even spare parts. Look at this piece of steel on my desk – it is part of a main battle tank's transmission. When we sell it to our foreign customers, we charge up to forty thousand dollars for this piece of stainless steel. I think that the true cost of manufacturing it is less than five hundred dollars, and this leaves a lot of money for both the kick-offs and profits. What other business, except illegal businesses and financial fraud, can provide such high profit margins?

You got all these nice tanks, trucks, armored vehicles, artillery, radar systems, communication systems, planes of all sorts, ships, submarines, rockets, and so on. They all need to be maintained, and it all comes at a price. An army needs to be clothed and fed; here you have additional profit opportunities. Flying a plane or driving a tank requires fuel which also comes at a price. The barracks and military bases need maintenance too, they need construction work too. If you build an underground base, who can tell how much it really costs? All military systems, though often made of durable materials, become technologically obsolete after a while. One has to introduce new weapons systems at regular intervals, regardless of whether or not the previous generation of weapons got used or not. All the day to day equipment a military uses, like vehicles and trucks, are just like vehicles civilians use: They break down and they need to be repaired and maintained. Any serious military is such a huge complex of items which all need to be manufactured, maintained, and replaced, that nobody really knows how much it truly costs. If anyone really asks, one can always say that it is a state secret and no information needs to be provided. Any real military is a gigantic cash cow that provides unimaginable wealth to those who control it. This is why humanity will probably never get rid of it."

"This is enlightening Sir, are all the countries of the world similar in this way of treating the military as a gigantic cash cow?"

"Not all. They differ of course. There are many countries, especially in the developing world, which allegedly have strong militaries on paper. Most of the officers in these countries are incompetent; they are officers because they are someone's relatives. Their weapon's systems are not maintained and spare parts are stolen and sold to other countries in order to make profits. Never look at the sheer numbers when looking at military capabilities."

"Does this mean that countries that are military paper tigers could be taken out by a small professional military?"

"Absolutely. You take a thousand special forces operatives, add several hundred high precision missiles to knock out key military and communication facilities, provide two dozens of very capable fighter jets with top gun pilots to command the air space, and you can defeat a country of say, twenty million people. You can defeat them, but you cannot hold them! You cannot occupy them with such forces."

"I understand. It becomes clear that there is a huge difference between defeating someone militarily and occupying the same country."

"Exactly, this is the case. To occupy any country means to be in day to day contact with the general population. In the majority of cases, this means outright friction. All it takes for the locals is to have small groups of patriots who oppose the occupation. If these people are smart and if they keep their mouth shut, they will torment the occupier in very frustrating ways. The occupying force will inevitably retaliate, meaning civilians get killed and the whole affair becomes biblical. Before you know it, millions of people literally hate the occupier force and wish to see its destruction. This is all known. Hence, the old ways of simply subduing a foreign country by military means are less and less practiced today."

"In your opinion, what will be the future of military confrontations in the not so distant future?"

"The people in your Institute would know the answer to this question better than I do. I can provide you with my personal opinion only. I do not think that we will see much of the classical confrontations of the type of two big armies fighting a war on a battlefield. The disproportion between the actual capabilities of the different countries is such that most of the conflicts will resemble the ancient story of David versus Goliath. Currency and trade wars will again be predominant. Thinking of wars in general, we may witness invisible and hard to prove wars."

"What are invisible and hard to prove wars?"

"The human being has limited sensors. Our understanding of the world is in four dimensions. It is length, width, height, and the fourth dimension being time as we comprehend it. The world is vastly more complex than just these four dimensions."

"Please continue."

"The ultimate way of imposing one will over the other is to do it invisibly, without evidence of any involvement. Let us say, there is continuous drought or floods in the territory under control of your potential enemy. This weakens your enemy, makes the enemy realize that it is better to compromise than to fight. Even if the enemy suspects that you are behind the sudden mishaps, but they cannot prove it, he will not be sure of it and will decide to compromise. Think of another scenario, stage after stage, the masses of the people start to change their minds and start to accept what you want them to accept – due to delicate and gradually introduced propaganda. The whole process is peaceful, and there are almost no violent events at all. Everyone considers that this change of attitude, this newly found acceptance, happened on its own – that it is part of the development of the society. A few minds will speak against it because they suspect foul-play. However, these critics are easily marginalized, obscured, and otherwise silenced. They can even be of help. You give them some carefully engineered media coverage, and the general public gets the impression that they are nothing but a bunch of amusing and crazy people. This even strengthens the belief of the masses that they, the masses, know what's going on. The people start doing what you want them to do, and the people are content and happy while doing it. Is this not the ultimate weapon?"

"Do such weapons exist?"
"There was significant research conducted in exactly such fields of interest. Whether such weapons exist is something I cannot tell you. If they exist it would be classified. My role is to point you in the directions needed to open your mind to the possibilities."

"Sir, I thank you very much. You gave me a lot of insights that are new to
me."

Just as spring was unfolding in late April of 1994, Sol's Russian
experience came to its end. He had seen and lived a life in a world that
was very different from his preconceived ideas of Russia and its people.
He had made real friends, enjoyed cultural events, had plenty of modest
dinners filled with lots of heart and humor, and, at the same time, learned
from knowledgeable people. His transformation had been rapid, and he
had matured considerably during his time in Russia. Sol now understood
why the Institute had made it mandatory for potential analysts to go
through a definitional mission before employment. Partly it was to
exemplify the stark differences between textbook knowledge and reality.

Having completed the first part of his mission, he packed his suitcases and
his journey continued.

EXPERIENCING WAR

April 2, 1994, Zagreb, Croatia

Sol arrived at the Zagreb Intercontinental hotel in the evening hours. While he was checking in, the receptionist gave him a note stating – Opera bar, Mr. Horvat. Upon leaving his suitcase in his room, Sol went to the 17th hotel floor. The view of the city lights was a sight worth memorizing. The waiter led Sol to a corner table where his local Mentor, a seasoned gentleman in the mid-60s, waited for him.

"Good evening, Mr. Horvat, it is a pleasure to meet you."

"Good evening, Sol. How was your experience in Moscow? Your future boss briefed me about your travel, and the purpose of it being to open your mind to the many facets of our world."

"I am still processing everything that I learned in Moscow. It is indeed different from what I thought it would be. It is true that having been someplace is different than having only thought or read about it."

"Yes, this is true. This brings us to your task in this part of the world and my role in it. Tomorrow at 0800 hours you will be picked up by a small United Nations observer team that is going to the war-torn areas of the region. You will do exactly as you are told, and there will be no problems regarding your safety. The war has moved from Croatia to neighboring Bosnia and Herzegovina. A third of Croatia is occupied, lots of infrastructure is destroyed, we have hundreds of thousands of refugees we take care of, and some towns are still being shelled by artillery on a daily basis, but we do have a sort of a temporary armistice."

"Sir, it is a great view from this bar. Looks beautiful, all the city lights, glimmering, I would never say that this country is at war. The front lines are perhaps some 50 kilometers from here."

"As I just told you, the war has moved eastwards. It was very intense in this city two years ago, but right now it is safe."

"What can I expect when I am in the field?"

"The UN observers have access to most of the sites where military activity is taking place. Prepare to witness the ugly reality of war. It is hard to explain war to someone who has never seen it. You have four weeks to learn about war, and what it means to the people as well the economies of the involved countries. Always remember how lucky you are for just being an observer. Observe and learn, that is your task."

"Mr. Max said that I will be able to learn from you about certain 'specifics' about war, and how a functioning society can collapse in a very short period of time. When will I have a chance to ask you questions?"

"Not today. Think about your Moscow experience. You came to Moscow with some weltanschauung of your own and left it with another worldview. Is it not so?"

"Yes Sir, as I stated, I am still processing all the information gained in Moscow."

"If we were to talk about war today, we would be wasting valuable time, young man. Upon your return, we will spend a whole afternoon together and then we can talk about your experience."

"Understood, it makes sense. If you don't mind I would retire now and get some decent sleep before tomorrow's early start."

"Please do so, but before you leave, let me just give you a brief explanation. War is an unfortunate affair. It has a profound and deep impact on most people. War has a dynamic and a life on its own. It is a very specific event."

In the following four weeks, Sol witnessed a myriad of things and events. He was at the front lines and slept in improvised shelters. He experienced the sound of battle, saw the magnificent manifestation of artillery duels on the horizon in the dark of night – it looked like the God of War – Mars, had arranged gigantic fireworks.

Getting real close to the realities of war, he visited refugee camps, saw prisoner of war camps at a distance, and walked through a morgue filled with corpses; he would forever remember the sweetish smell of dead bodies – something all soldiers remember for a lifetime. Looted and burned villages, destroyed bridges, trenches, artillery positions, outposts, hospitals filled with wounded people, most of them younger than Sol was – all of these left a lasting impression on the young apprentice. War is a profound experience, and it began to take a toll on Sol. Having spoken to and seen disturbed, desperate, and completely lost victims of war, different types of soldiers and paramilitary figures, strange uniforms, violent people, the mentally ill, drunkards, and addicts – slowly but surely, his experiences became heavy weighs on his shoulders that psychologically manifested themselves as depression and melancholia.

Man-made atrocities leave a lasting impression.

At the end of his experience, Sol did not speak as much as he used to do, and observing his reflection in the mirror, he could count more and more gray hairs. Even though he had not been involved in the war, it had left scars in him.
After four weeks, Sol returned to Zagreb and enjoyed the comfortable amenities the hotel had to offer. Immediately after checking in, he went to bed and slept for nearly 20 hours when the phone rang and Mr. Horvat asked him whether he would join him for an afternoon walk and lunch.

This was the moment Sol had waited for. This was the chance to summarize his recent experiences and ask a few questions in order to round-up his war experience. At noon, Sol met Mr. Horvat at the hotel lobby. It was a beautiful spring day and the gentlemen walked through the

18th and 19th-century built town. The architecture was similar to that of other central European cities. Sol learned that it was 900 years since the name of the city was first mentioned, and that the history of this country was marked with many wars and invasions of the past. Interestingly, the last military attempt of Islam to conquer Europe was brought to a halt in this region, and since it meant 400 years of consecutive defensive war, it was obvious that people here had suffered greatly for a long period of time. Zagreb's cathedral was a special treat, really beautiful piece of neo-Gothic architecture. Its twin towers as tall as the Saturn Five rocket that brought mankind to the moon. After two hours of casual walk and talk about history, culture, music, and life in general, the gentlemen settled in a small restaurant overlooking the city, just a few hundred meters from the nation's parliament.

"Mr. Horvat this is an excellent restaurant, it feels like being in the midst of nature, yet we are in the very center of the city. From what I've seen, it is a nice city, and I am stunned with the peace and tranquility I could see on the streets and the many café bars, after all, this country is at war."

"War affects people in different ways. I thought this would be a good setting to listen to your questions and give you some answers. What is your impression of war?"

"I am deeply depressed with what I have seen. All this tragedy is hard to process. In university I read about many different wars, contemplated and analyzed various aspects of them, and I wrote essays about wars in my history class, but now that I have seen just a small fragment of a war, I am terrified."

"I told you that it is an unfortunate affair. People who are involved in war events are reasonably preoccupied with it. To think about war without having seen it is futile."

"Why do people fight in this war?"

"Well, there are different reasons, of course. Those who are drafted, fight because they have no choice. People who lost a dear one or lost property, these people fight for reasons of revenge. Professional soldiers fight because it is their job; it is the same with mercenaries. Then there are all sorts of deranged people, adventurers, psychopaths, and really vicious characters who love war and enjoy the opportunities of pillage and brutality. This affects all sides of the conflict. I do not know how much time you had to follow world events during the past four weeks. There is actually a much more brutal affair happening as we speak."

"I did not watch any television nor did I read any newspapers. What can be more gruesome than what I have just seen?"

"Rwanda. It looks that up to a million people got killed in a matter of weeks. One tribe organized a mass slaughter of another tribe. Their weapons of choice were machetes. Someone calculated that every 11 seconds a person got slaughtered. It is one of the most efficient cases of organized genocide in known history. These folks were more efficient than the Mongols, and the trouble has not ended."

"What?! I haven't even heard of this until now. I was fully focused on the slaughter going on in this part of the world. I am glad my definitional mission did not include Rwanda!"

"The Blue Helmets were there too, but they were not allowed to get involved. The UN is there to divide the conflicting parties, not to intervene."
The waiter brought a big plate with various foods and a bottle of quality red wine.

"Sol, let us enjoy our lunch. While doing so, please think about equality. I understand that your questions will lead into the directions of why this or that has happened. In order for me to be of help, I ask you to think about the questions of equality. Let me improvise a bit. Look at these two wine glasses on our table. They are manufactured items and are basically identical. Just because they are identical does that entitle them to equal destinies? Or look at those poplar trees outside. They all belong to the same family of trees. Does that entitle them to identical, equal destinies? Think a bit about this while we eat. Then I will try to explain you one of the facets of society that is important in understanding why and how some events happen. This is related to the question of why wars happen.”

Sol was pondering what do poplar trees have to do with wine glasses and why would this have anything to do with wars? The food was very delicious and so was the wine. As they finished with the main course, both gentlemen felt very comfortable and were ready to continue with their conversation.

“Sol, wars occur for many reasons but seldom, if ever, do they just happen. There are different conditions that lead to war and one of them is the mood of the public.”

“We learned about it at the university. Are you addressing propaganda?”

“Propaganda is part of the total package. What I am addressing has much to do with the wars fought in this region of Europe at the end of the 20th century. In the past five decades, there were serious efforts by the local powers-that-be to promote the concept that all people are equal and that they, the people, are automatically entitled to certain rights because all are equal. There is no way that all can be equal, just because they belong to the same species. These two poplar trees outside of the restaurant may share common traits, but one will die sooner than the other, one consumes more water than the other, and there is no way to guarantee an equal destiny to those two trees. In the case of the human species, it is even more complex. The idea that all people are equal is a construct that can have a lot of appeal, especially with the less educated folks. For a while, a government can introduce laws that guarantee many equal rights, they can subsidize whole industries and artificially create workplaces, pay salaries that have not been earned, distribute bonuses and benefits to everyone because all are equal – this can go on for a while. Unless this is closely backed up by a sustainable economic model, a moment comes when such a society can no longer be sustained. There is no money for it, and compound interest shows its ugly face."

"I am getting the point Mr. Horvat. This region has also pursued, even quite successfully a socialist path, accelerated industrialization of the nations that comprised the former federation, accelerated production of higher education degrees, free housing, and much more. And this system went bankrupt."

"Yes. The golden age of the former federation lasted perhaps 10 years; it was during the 1970s. In order to keep this multinational federation intact, a significant sum of borrowed money got spent in ways to buy popular peace. The citizens were preoccupied with a rising life standard and got used to it. However, investments did not yield enough revenue to benefit industry to be really competitive.

After 1980, the consequences of such policies became evident. Different reforms, stabilization measures, devaluations of local currency, and deflation and inflation became the new reality of the day. Money got spent but it was not spent wisely. It got spent with the short term objective of assuring social peace. In the 1980s, the old issues, the different histories of the different nations that were part of the Yugoslav federation, started to resurface. The economic hardships brought old grievances to life. The federal government could not agree on real solutions to this problem and because of geopolitical reasons, they could not attack a neighbor and divert the public from economic woes through a manufactured war. The one-party political system was incapable of reforms, and the cohesion was lost. Some tried to impose their will on the others by means of military threat, and others started to boycott the bully by means of withholding their economic power. As a result of poor governance, the conditions became such that a war between the different nations, comprising the federation, became a reality."

"If I understand correctly, this is another case where economic reasons triggered a war? Was the propaganda strong in this region? Did they brainwash people?"

"The propaganda was indeed very strong and thorough. People were made to believe that they were special, and that the domestic system of governance and the economic model were the best that could be. It was continually emphasized and underlined that there were powerful external, and sometimes internal enemies, and for these reasons, all the nations of the Yugoslav federation had to be united in order to prosper.

Additionally, the system knew how to be oppressive; the security apparatus was quite robust, and in some earlier days of the federation, you could end up in a concentration camp for political prisoners. At the same time, there were real improvements felt by the masses. This gave the system the needed trustworthiness. As it goes, people wanted more and more. Unfortunately, the economic model was not as efficient, and it could not pay for all the wishes the general public had. Once it became obvious that the economy was in a decline and then in a free fall, the trustworthiness of the system was gone. Hereafter, old grievances and the language of hate started to appear. It all ended in a war among the republics that formerly had comprised the federation."

"It all makes sense, Mr. Horvat. Big promises that are not kept lead to even bigger disappointments. Interestingly, you place quite some importance to this topic of equality. I understand that it was a communist socialist system, which always follows the rather similar agenda of redistributing the wealth among the people based on the notion that all people are equal. It looks like this cannot work, or can it?"

"There is never enough wealth to satisfy everybody. What is doable is to create the conditions for the creation of new wealth, and this new wealth is distributed along some lines of equal rights and equal needs. But this requires a highly disciplined, highly ethical, and highly productive society – led by a very efficient and righteous government. Only a few nations could actually pursue such a path. Central government and governments in general are not really good at creating new wealth. Governments can create the legal conditions and incentives that lead people who have some capital, some skills, and the entrepreneurial talent to take the risk and, thus, create new wealth. If such conditions are not there, if the system is corrupt, taxation high, and incentives exist only on paper, then you will never see sufficient business success stories that can create sufficient new wealth. I repeat: only a few nations could afford such a system in which almost everyone is taken care of – fairly. The big majority of nations can only sell utopian dreams to their people and perhaps achieve short periods of economic prosperity before it all ends up with a dystopian reality. In the end, the conditions in the society get even worse than they have been before someone sold utopian and populist agendas to the masses. Propaganda is the tool used to make the general public believe in something that does not exist.”

“Mr. Horvat, it seems that this war can be classified as a case of implosion. The problem could not be exported, there were no potential victims who could be attacked and plundered, so the problem could no longer be contained and ended up in an internal war.”

“Yes, you can use such a definition for this particular war. In life, there is only one way of doing things, one path to follow that has realistic chances of achieving the desired objectives. It applies to governments and nations as much it applies to a single person. There is only one proper way of doing things – everything else is too extreme.”

“Sorry, what is the proper way of doing things?”

“Does the name Siddhārtha Gautama sound familiar to you?”

“The Supreme Buddha”

“That gentleman identified it clearly. The only proper path is the middle path. This is the balanced path. It takes wisdom and experience to truly understand it. It works in everything from private life, business life, love, war, and in all of human affairs. The moment one goes too much left or right, up or down, one enters the world of extremes. And this is common to governance as well. A balanced economic model, a bit of all the capabilities but not dependent upon any particular single niche is a very good basis for a good economy. Good governance means not too much of anything, yet sufficient thorough control over those issues which could lead to catastrophic outcomes. Societies that follow this path never have too much of anything, yet they have everything they need. Communism would require ethical leaderships and highly conscious citizens with a very strong sense of ethics for all of it to work out properly. Democracy also requires capable leaders plus a mature population. If one does not have these elements, the middle path is lost and the whole affair goes astray."

The waiter brought the restaurant's specialty – pancakes of the sort Sol had never tasted before. Though the topic of discussion was serious the atmosphere at the table was one of peace, understanding and creativity.

"Mr. Horvat, if I may ask. What was your position in the former federation? Mr. Max mentioned that you were an international diplomat. Why do you currently work for the United Nations and not for your country?"

"I am a citizen of the world and a professional who knows how it functions. I am not interested in selling utopian and populist dreams to the masses while enriching myself through the accelerated privatization of state property. I am happy with my work for the U.N. since they appreciate the skills and experience I have."

"Privatization, you say. This topic is very much relevant and alive in Russia as well. It all looks like outright theft. What are the main benefits for the masses in the formerly communist states of Central and Eastern Europe that are now transitioning to capitalism – I mean the transition from a one party system to a democracy?"

"The majority of people undergoing this transition will become very poor, and their countries will be very weak as a result of the privatization of state assets without any real investment into new workplaces and competitive capabilities. The one party system is being replaced by a two party system, but the real problems of the societies will not get solved at all. The people will gain one thing only, guaranteed by law."

"What is this one thing?"

"The right to vote is the only thing that they will gain."

"Is there anything else that you can tell me about the reality of the nation state? Issues that are not understood by the general public, indicators perhaps?"

"If you are a major power, you do not need to win any wars, all you need to do is to disturb those that have the potential of becoming a peer power. You interrupt their development before they threaten your unilateralism. Major powers can afford to wage expensive wars without victory because in the long run, they are victorious."

"If the bureaucrats start to view themselves as privileged, instead of being public servants with an assured monthly paycheck, it will result in a decline of the economy. The more bureaucracy there is in a state, the less competitive the economy is. In the end, private businesses are nearly completely eliminated in a country where the bureaucracy has gotten out of control. Eventually, since nobody is engaged in any productivity and original ways of creating new wealth, the bureaucracy starts to eat-up itself. The only way for such bureaucracy to survive is the creation of an extremist state, something along the lines of fascism. If this is not possible, the whole system implodes like it did here."

"The biggest of all lies ever told is that we are all equal. Wherever you see this being said or even used as part of an ideology – do know that no good will come out of it! People are not equal; they never have been and never will be. People are different!"

"Mr. Horvat, many thanks for your kind time and attention."

The two gentlemen left the restaurant and observed the sunset from the nearby vista before their paths parted. Sol spent another night in a transitional economy, an unfortunate country at war. He was happy to know that his life was safe. His youth had not been consumed by war, and he had a future worth living. Three months was all it took for his definitional mission to be completed, yet it had had a major impact on him and had changed him forever. As experienced by Sol, there is a vast difference between observable or practical reality and that which can be accessed through textbooks and television.

THE RELIEF

May 2, 1994 – The Institute, Switzerland

Sol was overwhelmed with the sight of the Institute. How tranquil, beautiful and peaceful it was. He immediately went to report to Mr. Max.

"Good afternoon Sir!"

"Good afternoon Sol, welcome back. How was your definitional mission?"

"It was mind bending, inspiring, depressive, and sometimes also quite dynamic. Now I understand the great difference between theory and practice. My worldview has changed. I have made so many conclusions yet even more questions to ask myself!"

"Excellent. Am I to suppose that you still want the job with the Institute?"

"Absolutely! I would like to sign the contract right away. I thought it over many times and wish to thank you and the Institute for this great opportunity."

"Well, here are four copies of the contract and a pen. You have already read it previously. Please sign here. You can keep the pen as a souvenir."

Sol signed the contract with the Institute. Now his life had a firm, professional direction.

"Sol, I got some work to finish right now. Please check with my secretary, and she will give you the keys to your apartment. The definitional mission reporting and accounting can wait. Let us meet in three hours at the restaurant for a conversation."

Having settled in his new apartment, he showered, shaved, and put on his best suit. Sol's mood was excellent when he arrived at the restaurant. A few minutes later, his Boss arrived.

"Do you understand the reason why we have sent you on this definitional mission?"

"Yes. Compared with all the teachings and tons of books, the reality in the field does look very differently. There is a lot of despair and pessimism that cannot be felt in theoretical ways. To have been there absolutely makes a difference."

"Yes, the reality of the human species can be very cruel."

"Sir, the majority of people figure out what is happening only after it happened. There are always people behind the scenes who are the puppet masters."

"Yes, the wizards behind the curtain. Most of what the masses see, hear, and believe are illusions. There are many elaborate hoaxes out there. For example, there is no doubt that mankind is polluting the environment. Remember what I told you about climate change? Climate change is visible, but is it really exclusive to human-made pollution or is it perhaps a normal occurrence resulting from complex activities of the sun and the universe? If it is the sun and the universe, then there is nothing we can do about it. But we do not know the truth, do we? Some people do know the truth, but cannot share it with the general public for many reasons. What was most intriguing to you?"

"The fact that everything revolves around the economy was so visible. Many of the locals blame the hardships of the transition period on the Western governments and businessmen. They often said that the various academics and aid assistants who ostensibly came to help had no clue about what to do."

"This is indeed a tricky issue. There is always more than one side to every story. From a legal aspect, all these transitional countries are sovereign. The very transition from one economical system to another is always painful and takes time. Business people will look for opportunities – but that does not necessarily mean that their actions are orchestrated by a foreign government. Some of these events, for example the collapse of an industrial giant like the Soviet Union, is without precedent, and there is no historical sample to learn from. Last but not least, many of the locals in positions of power are certainly not interested in reforms because they realize the opportunity to increase their own wealth. Under such conditions, one can send the brightest minds to help them, yet without any positive results."

"Mr. Max, I will need some time to process all what I have seen and heard. I realize that the product of the Institute has to include many realistic facts that are often brushed aside for being politically incorrect or otherwise not presentable."

"Sol, our clients are not interested in political correctness. Our clients are interested in our product being as accurate as possible. Never be fooled as an analyst. As an analyst one cannot be an idealist. We can have wishes, and we may dream about a better world, but such thoughts may not show up in our work. Some things that you have seen or heard will take time for you to truly understand. You start as an apprentice with us, and all you need to do, during the first years, is not to question the judgment of our senior members. Because you now understand that the realities of the world, there is no need for endless arguments and explanations. Our senior members are experienced in the ways how this world really functions. Learn from them, pay attention to details, and your part of the work will contribute to our end-product being professional and accurate. It is very simple."

"Yes Sir, I accept that there are many different realities."

"Sol, there are many, many different realities. Modern science is dealing with possibilities that our reality is nothing but a hologram, and that it has nothing to do with what we consider to be reality. Our work at the Institute is interesting because we have to take into account many different details, many different realities in order to provide good service to our clients. Putting numbers together behind a comfortable desk in our Institute does not suffice. Your definitional mission exposed you to the subtle differences that are ever present. Now you should be open-minded to accept that there are many factors that we need to take into account before we come to any reasonable conclusion or recommendation."

"Thank you Sir, thank you for your trust and opportunity."

"Sol, welcome to the family, now you are one of us!"

CHAPTER 3:
THE ASSIGNMENT
(2018)

Everything in the world may be endured except continual prosperity

Johann Wolfgang Von Goethe

The 21st century did not start as many people had hoped it would. Those who enjoyed prosperity started to realize that nothing could be taken for granted. The Western world was busy with capital market destructions and the dismantling of the welfare state. The rest of the world was preoccupied with intentions to reach higher levels of prosperity, often not understanding that much of everything is interconnected. Wars became wars without an end in sight. The world of finance was moving in seconds, and science & technology started to introduce major breakthroughs every six months. The world of business maintained its pace in weeks, months, and years. Societies were not catching up with this accelerated trend at all.

Citizens of welfare states gradually began to learn that such states are dying faster and faster every day. The human rights agenda lost its meaning since, without income, people cannot exercise any rights at all, regardless of what is promised in some document. Hundreds of millions of families began descending into the abyss of eternal poverty, where they are about to join the billions who never knew anything else but abject poverty. It is, of course, much harder to descend than to climb a mountain. Those born in poverty could hope that they will, somehow, see improvements to their life standard. Those descending into poverty had no real reason to hope for anything.

Sol appreciated the work at the Institute. He did not have to commute, and his earnings were decent and regular. The actual job became a routine of numbers, analyses of processes, and estimations of the varieties of likely outcomes. The computer power of the Institute combined with the presence of knowledgeable people became Sol's creative environment in which he felt secure. The Institute maintained its competitive edge in these times of certain uncertainty.

THE MOTIVE

On the 11th day of January 2018, one of the former clients came to a private visit to the Institute. In the vista rich office at the top of the Institute's main building, Mr. Max opened the meeting.

"Sol, it is a pleasure to introduce you to one of our most important past clients. Mr. Goodwill is the former CEO of one of the biggest pension funds in the Western world. He came for a private meeting and asked me to bring my most diligent project manager to the table, and you are my choice. Let us listen to what the interest of Mr. Goodwill is."

Mr. Goodwill stretched in his comfortable chair and raised both hands, showing the quote – unquote signs before he started to talk.

"Gentleman, I made good money in the times when I needed expert advice as a CEO of a trillion dollar pension fund. Let us go back in time. Around 1989 as the Cold War ended, some guilds were able to capture the moment and introduce a strong impetus that would change the world as we know it. Western finance introduced new business concepts, created new products, and lobbied for major changes in legislature that were in place since the Great Depression of the 1930s. The result was an open, global market in which the power of money could move undisputedly at the speed of light. The world of finance used the technological advances to a much higher extent than most other guilds known to humans. As a result, money could be created faster and in greater quantities than ever before. This has shaped the world in ways that are unprecedented. By 2008, I did realize that all the mathematical models and predictions that I have received from your Institute are correct. Listening to your advice was the smartest thing in my professional life. I am glad that I switched the focus of our fund to tangible assets, like natural resources and long term lease contracts of fertile lands, around the world. At the time I was doing it, nobody understood it, and I was subjected to great criticism and foul play. Today we have motion pictures and documentaries that portray what has happened in the autumn of 2008 and almost all estimated that the music has stopped, which it did. For the past 10 years, the dance has continued based on the echoes of the music that played in the past, but the echo itself is fading. I retired a few years ago and was proud to not have lost the life savings and pensions of millions of citizens that entrusted their livelihood to the fund I managed. I exited the ballroom with honors and retired to the countryside. For the first time in 30 years, I had time for my family. Quietly observing what is happening in the world of today and having the future of my grandchildren on my mind, I came to some conclusions which motivate me to do one more thing. It is my wish to launch a product that should help the young generations, starting with the Millennials, to better cope with whatever life throws at them. The world is accelerating and people have hard times catching up with it. Knowledge is becoming obsolete at an accelerated rate. Your Institute may help me in this endeavor."

All three gentlemen exchanged views and started thinking deeply about the subject. Mr. Max gave an eye signal to Sol, authorizing him to continue the discussion.

"Mr. Goodwill, we may again offer honest advice to you. Can you tell us more?"

THE OBJECTIVE

Mr. Goodwill stood up and started to walk around the conference table.

"I have compiled a list of features, a list of characteristics that I wish to see included in the product which this Institute should create:

1.   It has to be doable with technologies available today or in the nearest future with the target introduction date of the solution being around the year 2025.

2.   It has to be easily accessible and easy to use. Something that does not require a long learning curve. Don't forget that people no longer read much, if they ever did. Thus, it has to be as simple as possible.

3.   It has to be a free product. Every person should be able to use it. I have a team of experts that know how to make a product available for free.

4.   It has to be useful. Something that the masses will not use for self-gratification and ego-trips. Something that they can actually use for their own and then also for the benefit of the society as a whole.

Sol wrote the four listed features on a piece of paper and replied:

"Mr. Goodwill we will follow your outlined priorities. If you would summarize, what should this product do for the masses?"

"I seek a product that will help people accept their own destiny more easily and accept the realities of life. It has to help humans better cope with their lives and the world around them!"

There was a pause after Mr. Goodwill summarized what he is seeking. Sol felt insecure, and his Boss noticed it and took initiative:

"Mr. Goodwill, we have to be absolutely realistic about this objective. We all know that the world is a very diverse place. The situation faced by people is different from continent to continent, not to mention all the other differences based on age, social status, knowledge, health, and so on. Different cultures, different situations, different destinies all together. Everyone needs a roof over his head, clothing, water, food to survive, and, hopefully, a few items more to live. I do not think that you are seeking a product that could solve all these needs and resulting problems?"

Mr. Goodwill drew a box in the air with his fingers.

"I expect a product that will help people accept that they live in a box, meaning that they have no choice but to accept the limitations life imposes on them, and yet still get some happiness and joy out of living. Alternatively, the product should help people learn how to live outside of the box. The young generations live in a society where almost all that they say, watch, read, or write is permanently recorded. It is going to be very tough to find their place under the sun. That's the generation of my grandchildren, and I wish to use my financial assets to somehow help them all. I know it is a difficult task. What does our project manager think of it?"

Sol felt much more comfortable after Mr. Goodwill explained his wish in more detail. Sol then said:

"Gentlemen, I like the idea of the project because it is so different from our daily routines. Most of us were idealistic when we were younger. Then the realities of life forced us to abandon the idealistic impulses. I have some general ideas right now, but they are too vague for anything specific. I am certain that whatever we seek will be in the domain of internet and telecommunications. This is for the reason that what we seek has to be some kind of software implemented in the most user friendly and accessible hardware that is today. It certainly could use cloud technology. The general direction I would take is two-fold. One – we would conduct global opinion polls to better understand what people might need and accept. Two – I would like to take into account the ingenuity of the free thinking, creative minds who live and work right now. While we can find all sorts of ideas, concepts, and proposals in our own database, and among our core team at the Institute as well the hundreds of project-based associates, much of this is perhaps too much institutional. To create this product we definitively need to reach out to the free thinkers of our times – look in many directions and then summarize it in one easy-to-use product. We also have to take into account that this product will have to work under the conditions of a controlled Internet, as the days of relatively anonymous usage of the Internet are most likely behind us."

Mr. Goodwill again seated in the comfortable chair had two questions:

"When do you expect the Internet to become a regulated and controlled affair?"

Sol started to smile in the manner of a middle aged cynic.

"We don't know the exact date. There is too much free thought on the Internet – something like that is never tolerated for too long. The consolidation of Internet services creates monopolistic giants which in turn regulate and control things."

There was another pause of silence before Mr. Goodwill expressed another wish.

"Let us be pragmatic. We are witnessing a merger of several systemic problems, each of which is a nightmare on its own, but combined they are an overwhelming problem. Consumerism is not sustainable if it is to become the daily life-style of increasing numbers of people across the world. Automation and robotics are replacing human labor in ever increasing numbers. The ecological system is seriously degraded. There is no need to mention the deficiencies of the global financial system. All this leads to more and more friction and hate. A full scale nuclear war will most likely not happen, but there are many hot-spots where wars are being fought, and it appears that they might start spreading to several other areas. Think of a world where most of the civilizational advances and social services are drastically downsized or entirely gone. Think of a world in which smaller groups of survivors are attempting to endure life and build a new civilization. What sort of product would be needed to help the survivors make the best out of the challenging situations in which they would find themselves. This is then the fifth feature, I wish the Institute to include in this product ideation!"

Mr. Max silently applauded while rising from his seat and extending his hand to Sol.

"Sol, I wish you lots of fun with the creative chaos in front of you. Out of chaos comes order. I wish to talk with our client about the terms of business. Please excuse us."

Sol thanked Mr. Goodwill for the opportunity and left the vista rich office of his Boss. The business terms between the Institute and the client were never an issue for Sol. Mr. Max was the one who took care of business deals, strategic contacts, and a few other specific and interesting issues.

THE PREPARATION

Sol assembled his team who would work on the creation of Mr. Goodwill's product. The tasks and timeline were set. All work should be done within the remaining 11 months of 2018. Sol would take charge of the free thought element. He decided to personally meet free thinkers who were not confined to institutional thinking; he needed fresh ideas and neutral, non-biased opinions in order to identify the ingredients of the product. The secretarial office of the Institute conducted web research and identified several hundred free thinkers whose thoughts could contribute to the project. After getting in contact with each of them, the secretarial office explained the interest of the Institute and negotiated the terms of a potential collaboration. Some free thinkers agreed to an interview at a place of their choosing, which in most cases was the place of their work and residence. The majority of the free thinkers agreed to a videoconference call. The Institute would pay a reasonable fee for interviews lasting up to two hours, and the interviewees would sign a contract waiving any claims towards the Institute with regard to whatever potential results of their contribution towards the actual project.

Having negotiated the terms of the interviewees, the secretarial office started to look into the airline schedules. Sol had to visit six continents, and it was not an easy task connecting all the flights such that time and resources would not be wasted. His travel itinerary would start in February and end in March, after which there was enough time for additional meetings and consultations if the need would arise. While Sol was conducting the interviews, the team, responsible for creating the product, began researching global trends and potential technologies

THE VOYAGE AROUND THE WORLD

February 2, 2018, Frankfurt am Main, International Airport, Senator Lounge

Mr. Max and Sol shared their thoughts while waiting for their flights. Mr. Max had a scheduled meeting in South East Asia as part of his endless preoccupation with building first hand quality contacts with potential clients and other important world actors. Sol was waiting for his world travel to commence.

In the pristine environment of the Senator Lounge, the two gentlemen exchanged a few thoughts. Being the Boss, Mr. Max used the opportunity to point Sol to a few issues that could be of concern to his assignment.

"We have come a long way since we first met more than two decades ago. You developed into a prime quality researcher and product developer with excellent analytic skills. Are you happy with this assignment? I gave it to you because this is an opportunity to be idealistic, and I know that you have never lost the faith that the world could become a better place. This time you can really seek the solution regardless of what the mainstream trends and interests are."

"Yes, Max, thank you for the opportunity. I have some general thoughts about the eventual product, but I am really keen on listening to the people I am about to meet. Our analyses show that they are the most suited and freely thinking people at present. I will also have the chance to update my understanding of our world – seeing six continents in a few weeks, getting a feel of different cultures, and speaking to free thinkers."

Mr. Max reached into his attaché case and from it, he gave Sol an e-book reader and a charger.
"Here, have this with you. I've uploaded various ancient scripts and books on it. You will have lots of time on board the planes and in the airports.

Perhaps the contents of these old and modern non-mainstream texts can provide additional inspiration to you. Remember, the solution to any complex problem is usually very simple. There have been billions of humans before us, there have been different civilizations before our civilization, and we are not the first ones who ask ourselves these questions. There is a solution for everything but one has to be open-minded and dare to venture into the realm of free thought in order to see the light. I like this project, and I gave Mr. Goodwill very favorable business terms. Whatever the Institute creates, we will contribute in-kind with our knowledge, computing power, and mathematical algorithms. Go and seek the solution. Be open-minded and don't worry about how much it may cost in monetary terms or whether the solution is opposite to the current mainstream trends. This time, you are free to be an idealist."

A few hours later, Sol observed the vastness of the Sahara Desert which constituted a separate world on its own. Our planet is so diverse. Life is so precious and fragile, yet it is capable of great accomplishments. Lying in the comfortable business class seat, enjoying the views and drinking quality wine, Sol activated the e-book reader he had received and started to review the scripts and books. It was a compilation of ancient scriptures and legends about the origin of man on our planet. It also contained various assessments about the future of mankind published by scientists and journalists in the 1970s and 1980s.

This assignment was surely the most thrilling of all the assignments Sol had since he joined the Institute. Not many have been privileged to get the opportunity to work on the identification of something that may help the people live in harmony with the world around it. It all seemed as a dream within a dream.

THE CONTINENT OF THE FUTURE?

05 February 2018 – Cape Coast, Ghana
Mr. Jonah, independent Sub Saharan African business developer

"Mr. Jonah, I read an article on the Internet in which you talked about Africa being the continent of the future. This is a rather ambitious statement. I came to ask you to tell me more about your vision."

"It is not a vision. You see, everyone says that the future of the world lies in Asia. The real great wars of the 21st century may be fought on that continent indeed. In regard to the long-term future, it is, however, not Asia where the real action will be. Sub-Saharan Africa is home to vast quantities of numerous natural resources and fertile land, plus there will soon be a billion people living on this continent. Most of them are hungry for the consumer experience. Thus, both the resources and the consumer markets are here – that is why I consider Africa to be the continent of the future."

"Mr. Jonah, this makes sense but there are open questions. How and with whom do the Africans intent to develop all these potentials? It takes money, it takes expertise to start something and eventually, it is a lot of hard work. All of this requires perfect organization and dedication. What about the political circumstances?"

"Yes, you put it well. Africa is not really different from other continents. Rulers who don't care about their people still exist and will exist. Any person using a cellular phone knows that it is manufactured in Asia. Much of the technology comes from America and Europe but many of the important materials for all popular gadgets come from Africa. The natural resources of all sorts are here. In order to access all the natural resources of Africa one has to build a transcontinental railroad that will span tens of thousands of kilometers in all directions. Railroads bring mobility. Along the railroads, new industries and businesses evolve. Shopping centers are necessary. You need roads too. Running water, sewage, water treatment plants, generation of electricity, power grids, and all of these have to be built. Airlines that connect the world with Africa and vice-versa with major hubs being in Africa, there are on the way. Housing, schools, and hospitals are certainly needed in sufficient numbers. All of these provide immense quantities of new revenue and new jobs. These jobs are not only African jobs – they are international jobs. We would like to activate our potential today. So far, we are witnessing progress happening."

"It is a great vision,. What is the backside of the African potential?"

"The backside is the fact that it is a big continent with lots of diversity and a rather absent interest of the wealthy Africans to actually invest in it and, thus, become even richer. Too much hope and expectation is placed on outside investors while life teaches us that if you want something done – you have to do it yourself!"

"Final question, Jonah, what do young people need in the world of today?"

"There are modern technologies that enable production. With these, we would have immense opportunities in online training and education. I think that the young generations should stop believing that the grass is greener someplace else. Instead, they should learn how to use modern technologies in a way such that the world comes to them instead of seeking luck and happiness far away from home."

THE RISING ECONOMIES

February 8, 2018 – Rio de Janeiro, Brazil
Mrs. De Sotta, blogger and macro-economist

"Mrs. De Sotta, you are known for your predictions about the economic development of world regions. I just arrived from Africa where I was presented with persuasive arguments that Africa is the continent of the future. What do you think, whom does the future belong to?"

"Mr. Sol, in the past decade alone, many books and essays got written about the tectonic shifts of the world economy. I am not addressing anything special that would not be known. The facts are often downplayed and ignored, but they are nevertheless facts and can be seen by a naked eye. Africa has a huge potential for development and so does Latin America. The bottom line is that it is a question of how long before the underprivileged, meaning the vast majority of any country, starts to question the lives of the privileged. Look around you. While we sit in a comfortable restaurant, we are surrounded by slums, or as they are called in Brazil, favelas. All around us are millions of poor people who live in miserable conditions. Whatever one does to improve their lives, one buys more time, more patience of the masses. A single light bulb in a household that never had electricity is a great and a visible incentive to the poor. Just a single light bulb that gives light in the night can make a lot of difference to people who never had it. The starting position of the great many is so low that it is not really a great task to make the poor feel that there is reason for hope. And hope is a strong and important element when you think about the human species."

"What about the advent of automation and robots? The world no longer needs huge pools of workers. How does this fit into your observations?"

"Yes, automation is a major game-changer, indeed. In regions with massive populations, labor will remain cheaper than automation."

"So, it is your opinion that the whole story about the rising economies, the so called BRICS is true? Might it not end up as a big bubble followed by a depression?"

"I have no illusions about that. It will certainly experience ups and downs, and there will be problems just like anywhere. One thing is certain: There are billions upon billions of whatever currency made among and between all those people who, until recently, could not make any deals. This has been going on for now, at least, twenty years and is hardly going to stop. No need to have some outsiders control and dictate the terms of business. This is a process that cannot be stopped."

"It cannot be stopped? Are you sure?"

"We already have very brutal financial wars going on. Currency wars are in full swing. Yet, the trend is unstoppable, and the big capital knows this and has already positioned itself in ways to make profits out of these new circumstances!"

"What should the young generations expect? What advise do you have for them?"

"They should not copy-paste success stories of others but should focus on their own in accord with the specifics of the place they live. They should observe and learn from others yet strive to identify and develop own solutions!"

THE CREATIVE HUMAN HIVE SOCIETY

February 12, 2018 – Orlando, Florida, USA
Mrs. Hamilton, retired professor of history and blogger

"Mrs. Hamilton, you write a lot about the human hive society of the future. This is a popular topic but your approach is different because you are not providing own opinion. You are compiling the many different visions, versions, and forecasts about the human society of the future as they were portrayed in books and motion pictures. I work on the development of products and wish to learn more about the possible future. What is your personal opinion about the society of tomorrow?"

"I am retired and reasonably well off, so I spend my time thinking about the likely social model of the future. It is a hobby of mine. The 20th century was very creative and productive in terms of literary arts and motion picture forecasts of the future. I do my best to read all such books and watch all the movies that have anything to do with the topic of the human society of tomorrow. First of all, there were always rulers and subjects. Some people were born into privileges and others into hardships. There existed no society that did not have some hierarchical order. In all of known mankind, there were always people who were materially, physically, mentally, and otherwise better off than others. No society is completely immune to corruption, whether it is political, monetary, or other form of corruption. Once these and many other eternal elements of society are accepted then one can look into the details. Disputing facts leads nowhere. It is not about whether I am right and you are wrong or whether there could be or was a better world. It is about how things are, and what is likely to come. Many consider that the future will bring a human hive society. I wish to think that it will be a creative human hive society."

"Of course, there are facts of life. What can a person living in the world of tomorrow expect? Is dictatorship the only future of such a world or is there a possibility of personal freedom and individuality?"

"This mainly depends upon the question of who designed it and who is in charge. If the only aim of such a society is to maintain absolute privileges for a small group of people then it is a dictatorial system, which gets frozen at a certain level of technological advance. There is no need for real inventions. There is no need for creativity. The basic requirements to sustain life remain the same for as long as such a system functions. It pretty much resembles the dull reality of today. People live the lives that are quite predetermined as they are born. Individualism has no place in such a society. This is the passive, status quo hive society. The other option is the creative human hive society."

"The creative human hive society maintains the option for individualism?"

"The creative human hive society of the future is one that has a creative objective. The order of things is maintained by providing the members of the hive with what they need and is reasonably affordable, while the system of values is such that individualism is not only allowed, it is stimulated. In order to achieve its ambitious, creative objective, the creators of the very society know that the human genius is unpredictable, and that the society always benefits from the talents and the creative power of its members. The status quo is still maintained even with very rigid measures. Disobedience is punishable with a death sentence. The members of the hive understand that there are things that are simply not asked because the answer is their own death. If life for the members of the hive is relatively bearable as it could be, the members see no incentive in death. Those who die due to punishment had to die because they posed a risk for the whole creative human hive society."

"Such a society has to get rid of poverty and has to provide adequate amenities to its members. In return, the hive protects itself from negative influences. I repeat, it does not have to be a dystopian hive society. It can be a creative one, but certain rules must be followed. The cornerstone of such a creative hive society is the actual objective of the society and the term of citizenship."

"Please elaborate."

"The objective of an ambitious hive society has to be reachable, yet without any reasonable time limit and no ending. There is no end result that tells that the quest of the hive society is over. There is a simple and easy to understand objective that serves the purpose. It is the colonization of the universe. Some results are obtainable within a generation, yet there is no ending as the universe is too big. This has been portrayed in many science fiction novels, and it bares two risks. One is the rebellion of the colonies in space, which can be avoided, while the other risk is that among the stars, a fierce enemy is encountered that brings so much trauma and horror to the creative hive society; thus, the whole quest is abandoned. Exactly such a scenario was also envisioned and written about many, many years ago. This is a technological objective of such a creative hive society. There could be spiritual objectives, too, i.e. that the whole society is involved in the quest of developing virtues. Such an objective can also have many checkpoints and achievements, yet the final objective is very far away and perhaps be unreachable. In any case, the objective is not to maintain a status quo of the society. The society's whole purpose is to achieve the objective, and this becomes undisputable."

"Please elaborate on the form of citizenship."

"Citizenship has to be earned. A truly creative hive society has to utilize the true creative as well productive potential of all of the hive members. For creativity and productivity to show, one needs opportunities. It is no secret that the age and experience of people do make a difference when thinking about responsibility, awareness of the potential of one's own action or inaction, the consequences, and many more details. A competitive and capable human hive society requires mature members who hold different positions of power or simply call it positions of function. This, too, is portrayed in motion pictures and it makes sense."

"How do you earn citizenship in a creative hive society?"

"At the age of 15, every member of the creative hive enrolls in a three-year-long program of serving the community. Unless puberty is eliminated, this takes care of the puberty-induced problems and hardships of the human species. One keeps the teenagers busy, and while doing it, one trains them and makes them understand how the creative human hive society functions. In the first year, the young help out in whatever services for the elderly; thus, the young learn something about old age. In the second year, the young help out in the technical maintenance of the infrastructure of the society; thus, the young learn about the requirement to maintain things if one wants the things to work. In the third year, the young help in administrative processes and, thus, learn the reality of administration and bureaucracy. As a reward, upon the completion of three years of service, each young person receives a nontransferable voucher for an around the world travel to them six inhabited continents with paid transportation, lodging, and food for a total of 180 days. Upon completion of their award travel, the young receive full citizenship and then comes their next step."

"What is the next step?"

"Their inclusion into the creative human hive society is the next step. The three year service that provides the right for citizenship adds much more information about every teenager. They all receive citizenship even if some teenagers require assistance in mastering the three year program. At the end of the citizenship program, enough knowledge about each new human hive citizen is collected and based on this knowledge further education, specialization, and, thus, position in the human hive society is determined. After gaining citizenship, the human hive collective invests into its citizens through education and training. This is why I call it the creative human hive collective because it does follow the concept of supporting the natural talents of every human hive member. The most talented gets picked first, the less talented are not left to rot on the streets. It becomes a multilevel process in which the creative human hive society invests resources and knowledge into its own future. There is a lot of individualism in all of this. Look at the way things are for the last several thousand years. It is not the creative potential; it is not the talent that really matters. Right now as we speak, hundreds of millions of people are performing some daily routines and jobs which they hate. The only reason they do it is because they think that they have no choice. There are so many talented people who are completely unproductive because the society has not yet evolved to the levels that make real sense. When people address the human hive collective as a dictatorial concept, people tend to forget that the world is a rather ugly and dull place during all of its known history."

"In your words, the human hive collective must not be a horrifying concept – it can be a creative and productive model of the society of the future, where everyone gets his fair share of work, food, shelter, amenities, and even the good feeling that comes when a person likes the life he or she is living?"

"The human hive society can indeed be a very nice society to be part of. Right now, most people have very little freedom. Their individualism is marginal and most of the world lives in a constant state of dictatorship. I mean, whom are we kidding?"

"If you would to summarize, what would be one of the essential elements of the creative human hive society of tomorrow? What would be one of the most defining reasons for such a society to perform properly?"

"Oh, that one is easy. A creative human hive society is based on real care of its members for each other. Especially in the case of the young, the young are coached and later educated by quality mentors. Whether it would be a completely digital system, like described in science fiction movies and books, or a human system of coaches and mentors that follow certain rigid standards of ethics and knowledge – this is open to speculation. But a successful creative human hive of tomorrow is based on real knowledge and wisdom. Without it, it is not possible to achieve it."

"Mrs. Hamilton, what is the role of the current generation of young people in terms of developing a creative human hive society?"

"Our world is again going through changes. Changes are part of life. Changes are a constant in the known universe. The challenges that lie ahead are immense, and it is questionable whether some old models of social order and organization can cope with the challenges of our times. Perhaps the young generations should ask for and seek a leadership that can enable the creation of a creative human hive society?"

THE COST OF BEING NAÏVE

February 14, 2018 – Atlanta, Georgia, USA
Mrs. Cobb, public relations advisor to Fortune 500 companies

"Mrs. Cobb, you are one of the most sought after public relations consultants. I work on a project that seeks ways to improve the competitiveness of young generations. When thinking about competitiveness, I came to the thought of being able to present oneself to the right people, sell the product to the right buyer, and things like that. Much has to do with how people see things, and, nowadays, much is related to public relations. Would you please tell me your opinion about the role of public relations in the world of today?"

"Public relations are as old as the beginning of man. It is just a different name for another less popular name, propaganda. The name propaganda became less popular because the whole thing got massively used prior to both World Wars by all sides. A lot of outright lies have been repackaged and sold to the naive public in order to make the general public agree with their destiny as cannon fodder. Some very smart minds gave it a new name and "public relations" got born. Different name - yet the same content. The eventual aim is to make others understand and do whatever you want them to understand and do. You have a plan but you don't want others to know about that plan and, at the same time, you want others to follow your plan though others should not know that there is a plan. How do you achieve that? The answer is public relations. You have a great message to share but are afraid that nobody will hear you. How do you fix that problem? Again, public relations will do the job. In general, public relations or propaganda serve the purpose of creating an impression. Good public relations can make a faulty product become a highly demanded item. Good public relations can help make other people do what you want them to do, without them knowing it. The real masters of propaganda can create a situation where the public suspects everything and believes in anything else but what you just told them. By wagging the people through different layers of propaganda, you can disorient them, make them tired and eventually they will accept almost anything you throw at them. Therefore, if you ask me how young people can be competitive, my answer is that they have to be shrewd. They need to be aware that almost everyone is using some sort of propaganda in his life."

"If propaganda or public relations is so frequent and can be very successful, then what is opposite of it?"

"Propaganda can actually be utterly lethal. Whole nations went to war because the nations believed in the stories and pictures provided by the propaganda machinery. This is lethal business no doubt about it. What is the opposite of propaganda? Well, that would be plain naivety. Did you not know that all of this is just a story? Did you not know that all of this is just a variation of the truth? Did you really think that this is the agenda, and you did not recognize what the true agenda is? Oh how naïve you have been. Naivety is on the opposite end of propaganda. The greater the lie – the more people follow it, said someone more than 70 years ago and it is true."

"What are the ideal tools for propaganda?"

"The ideal tools were always related to two things: a trustworthy source and the media by which propaganda is brought to the people. The ideal source is someone you trust. The ideal media is whatever media that does the job best. When thinking of mass propaganda, the best tool till the advent of television was radio. Television is a wonderful propaganda tool. In the past 60 years, television has created so many alternative realities that nobody can count them anymore. Television is both audio and video, you hear it and you see it. The next level is then the media that directly influences all of your thoughts and emotions. Eventually, mind control is the final propaganda tool."

"So television really has a major impact on people?"

"Of course it does. Think about the core nucleus family of the past. The adults diligently took care that the children behave properly, use the proper language, exercise politeness and respect when dealing with elders and so on. Then one day, someone brings this funny box into the household. In time, this box is allowed to misbehave all the time. It uses bad language, tells lies, spreads fear, and many more basically negative things, yet it is an accepted part of the household. It is even trusted. I would not take it if someone would give it to me! Oh, it's not free, it costs money. So people work to buy a TV set? Well, if this is so, then nobody should ask himself about the influence television has on the societies of the world. You can do your own programming, of course, and use the darn thing as a screen only. You watch what you want and when you want to watch it. But most people do not do it that way. For most people, television is their best friend. That tells us a lot!"

"If you think about the young people, the coming generations and the requirement for them to be capable to cope with the challenges of the world, what is one of the key skills or features they need to have if they are to be competent and competitive?"

"The young should not be naive. Naivety is lethally expensive!"

UNCHECKED CONSUMERISM

February 16, 2018 – Virginia, USA
Mr. Thomas, private entrepreneur

"Good afternoon Mr. Thomas, thank you for receiving me. A dear business friend of mine lost his job and soon his second marriage fell apart. He had to declare personal bankruptcy and was thinking of suicide. Then another friend of ours helped and sent him to you, paying for the treatment. Six months later, our mutual friend returned to Europe completely changed. He smiles, has found a new job, his second wife agreed to marry him again, and his children are happy. He is a changed man. I asked him what drugs he uses, and he said that there are no drugs but that there are changes in his worldview that made the difference. He would not tell me what you did to him and since you do not advertise your services, I came to ask you about your accomplishment. The reason for my interest comes from the task of my project in which I am seeking for ways to make people happier in their lives. Would you please extend me the privilege of telling me what is it that you do?"

"I will tell you about my work but you can only talk about it privately. I am not interested in publicity. My name is Jeff Thomas and I am a psychologist by profession who worked for some of the major corporations in their human resource departments. Five years ago, I decided to focus on excessive consumerism. I call it unchecked consumerism and developed a program, which helps those who can afford it, to change their lives. We run a six month's long program in the beautiful countryside of my home state of Virginia. Everyone calls our establishment the Happy Farm."

"So you help people change their habits?"

"It goes much deeper than that. We help people understand simple basics. To compete with those who inherited money and can afford many material things is an endeavor that is lost the moment you are committed to it. Copying the lifestyles of others can result in the total destruction of yourself and your family. Unless checked, consumerism in its most radical form can truly be compared with drug addiction. There are many similarities. Same as drugs are an escape from the actual reality, so is consumerism an escape from the reality of the consumer. It is an addiction. A drug addict will at some point commit crimes in order to obtain the money for the drugs he needs. An unchecked consumer will engage in more and more activities that can be considered as fraud, such as selling products that are faulty or services that are basically concealing their true criminal intent. For example, selling mortgages that will ruin other people. In order to satisfy the ever increasing hunger for more and more status symbols, one needs more and more money. There are high level theories and explanations that evolve around the fact that people emulate or imitate others, not considering that perhaps this emulation serves no purpose and perhaps they cannot even afford it. In the not so distant past, many motivated to obtain a higher education degree for reasons not limited to materialistic values only. People were satisfied that the higher education they were to receive would provide them with a secured future and better social status in the society. There were also ethical reasons, reasons of contributing to the society, helping others as an example. In the past 20 to 30 years, the whole concept is – everything counts as long it makes more and more money. Of course, this cannot end up well for most consumers, because their lives get emptied of all the actually important things which have been substituted with some items like vehicles, clothing, and membership in some consumer programs and so on. People imitate others instead of seeking satisfaction within themselves and their individual achievements that correlate with their own, actual reality. Consumerism is successful because it satisfies the many inner desires and wishes of the masses. Unchecked consumerism is directly linked with human vanity and pride. Instead of being proud of own achievements whatever they are, people project their pride in owning and using temporary items that for themselves say nothing at all. What car do you drive? Do you have the most recent clothing? Do you use brand B, it is popular this year? Oh, you use brand A which is out of fashion! These are simplified forms of what modern and unchecked consumerism does to people. Unchecked consumerism has destroyed valuable virtues such as spirituality, integrity of character, trustworthiness of a person and a sense for common needs of the society. Instead, unchecked consumerism promotes selfishness, arrogance, cut throat competition, and eventually ends in an empty world in which the individual is not connected to anything at all. We use the term unchecked consumerism, since consuming goods and services are part of daily life since the beginning of mankind. The hunters and gatherers were also consumers, but they did not focus on excess consumption. The consumption of goods and services is important to any form of economy, but there are limits to what is feasible. This is why we use this term – unchecked consumerism. In our workshops with patients who reached the level where one can actually talk with them, we analyze their individual lives. In most cases, they all lived rather decent lives. Had a roof over their head, had a regular and diverse diet, owned and used a reasonable car, had a job that perhaps was not the ideal of worlds but was much more satisfactory than the jobs they took later in order to afford their consumer addiction. People raised children, had some social life, were reasonably accepted in their society – in short, nothing spectacular, people lived decent lives they could afford. Then we looked how their lives changed once they decided, consciously or unconsciously, to commit to the exclusive path of unchecked consumerism. Eventually, they had no time, they were constantly tired, started to consume drugs that would help them stay alert, switched to jobs that they hated but made more money and in due process, they lost any contact with their children, their marriages broke apart, and they had more and more debt. Then one day, everything would fall apart. They realize now that the life they have lost was a beautiful life which they could afford. They understand now that once they are committed to the path of unchecked consumerism, they simply lived a life of nothing, or perhaps, of temporary satisfaction. One of the most common arguments we hear is that they wanted to be someone else and that they have seen the lives of others on TV, and that they would like to live such lives. Some people also frequently state that, in order to socialize, they had to copy the majority, thus, becoming unchecked consumers themselves. When we ask a simple question, such as, 'Do you think that all people can have everything, though their starting positions are different?' we get comments, like 'Life is unfair.' Of course it is, life is more often than not, unfair. The youth knows of no other world, and the youth emulates or imitates what they see from the older generations and, of course, the television. Only strong characters find the ability to admit to themselves that they were wrong about something, perhaps about everything. This is another workshop we have. We do our best to explain to our patients that they will feel better once they confront the reality for what it is. Again, this is a process. It does not come easy. There is no magic pill, which can raise the situational awareness of a person to levels required, within a few days. Strong individuals with receptive minds often take years to develop realistic situation awareness capabilities."

"What about the fact that no person can afford everything?"

"Yes, we use this term often. The responses are predominantly that people are provoked, and then ashamed if they cannot afford something. Rather than being ashamed, they will do anything possible to afford whatever it is that their social surrounding is asking for."

"I see, so it really is all about the worst of features within people. There is no shame if one cannot afford something. Simply don't socialize with people who demand of you the impossible."

"Of course you are aware that things are more complex. It starts with the elementary school. Children can be very brutal to each other. We all see children using cell phones that have features that perhaps you and I could use, not some third grade kid. It is hard for a child to defend his position in his world if he is laughed at by other children, because he does not have the latest model of a cell phone whose features no kid uses. You know that employers do like to have employees who are in debt, because this makes the employees docile. Much of society revolves around such basic differentiator factors. Fact is that many people who obtained some university degree remain quite limited. They are specialists in some field of human activity, if nothing else, on paper. This does not say anything about their intellect, whether they read smart books, or think that now that they have a certificate of sorts, they need no more education at all."

"Can you please tell me more about your anti-unchecked consumerism program, how it works, how you treat the patients?"

"We use similar methods like the anti-drug programs and sanatoriums combined. For those who can afford it, since we too need to cover the expenses and salaries of the personnel involved, we invite the patients for a six month's long stay at our farm. It is a big farm; we have farmland and grow potatoes and various vegetables we also consume. We have pastures with cows and sheep. We also have chicken, lots of chicken. There is a big chunk of woods that we own, so a bit of forestry work can be done. We show our patients how much work is needed to simply produce food and clothing products that we buy without any thought about where it all comes from. Our patients learn some basic skills, and depending upon the season, they even work in the fields. Like all programs that are designed to help people, we actually ask them to participate in work assignments. Our patients again learn how to socialize, how to be proud after a day of hard work, and to be satisfied with the results of their work. Many are alienated from mother nature. Many jobs show no immediate results, so we bring back the element of happiness that comes with the completion of an assignment. There are group therapies, just like in other programs. People do not discuss their alcohol habits but their consumer habits and what these eventually meant for their lives. We have absolutely no TV programs on our farm. Documentaries, comedies, and cartoons are what one can enjoy, that's all. We talk about natural resources, about the fact that perhaps a third of the world's countries consume many more resources than they can actually afford, unless they deplete the resources of those societies that have not reached the same levels of consumption. With natural resources we mean basics, like water, food, things like that. We don't go into uranium, oil, gas, and the likes. When people understand that water is precious, they start to think about it. An additional component is happiness. We ask participants how they feel when they have a simple influenza. Whether their only wish in that moment is to be healthy again?

Then we ask them, why not feel happy every time they wake up and can see, smell, walk, talk, think, feel, and breathe air?"

"You are reminding them of the very basics in life, yes?"

"Absolutely, this is one of the cornerstones of our effort. We make participants recollect that many of the best elements in life are free of charge; one only needs to be aware of them. We watch the sunrise and the sunset. When there are no clouds at night, we are amazing by the view of the stars in the sky above, just like they in the past. Most people nowadays live in urban centers, and they only see stars in science fiction motion pictures, and they are completely unaware that there are stars above them and that looking at them is a magnificent experience."

"May I ask about the results of the therapy and who pays the bills?"

"The program is now in its fifth year. We have had some 2,000 patients undergo the complete therapy at our farm. We maintain email communication with our patients if they want to. About 50% of our patients have changed their lives to the better, improved their social life, fixed the relations with their families, and readjusted their system of values. We are not against consumerism, as I explained, consumerism was always there. We try to help people get off the unchecked consumerism addiction which is ruining their lives and the lives of their families. In most cases, it is the family which pays the bill. Sometimes it is the employer who realizes that a good associate is in trouble and they invest in order to get the associate back to work. Just a small percentage of our patients pay the bill themselves. The majority tells us at the end of the therapy that this is the smartest money they have spent in years."
"You know, at the Institute I work, we have pastures and cows too."

"Well, whoever runs your Institute is obviously a smart person. Cows are important, the connection to mother nature is important."

"What do you think the young generations should understand about consumption?"

"It is simple. If you want a happy life, return to the basics, appreciate the real values and virtues. Avoid copying others and, by all means, do not become an unchecked consumer because it will destroy you!"

THE OBSOLETE EDUCATION

February 19, 2018, Washington D.C., USA
Ms. Madison, international educational consultant

"Ms. Madison, your recent book about the obsolescence of contemporary education met harsh criticism by the mainstream press, yet it was well received by the general public. You consider that in the majority of the world's countries, the educational system has completely failed. Why is that so?"

"Because it is only about the short-term business, and there are no long-term strategies present. Education has become an activity that dumbs down people and extracts as much money as possible from them. The system gives you some fancy diploma which, in most cases, is completely worthless. There is no real strategy or integration of the educational capabilities and capacities with the needs of societies and economies. In most places, the system is designed in ways to reward inefficiency and focus on the creation of many administrative jobs within the educational system itself. It is a self-centered system that only looks after its own interests, and as a result it produces shoddy products, like skills nobody needs, taught by theoreticians who, without real life experiences, teach about things that look very differently in the real world than in theory. In most places, the educational system has become an independent self-interest group, just like other interest-groups. It is not about quality; it is all about making as much money as possible in the shortest amount of time. No visions, no trustworthiness, and no guarantees are provided by most of the educational systems, right now."

"Are there any positive samples of proper education happening as we speak, someplace, somewhere on our planet?"

"There are positive sample cases. but these are limited to smaller nation states who still maintain the logical national interest of taking care of their own functioning society. These positive sample cases are an exception and there are not many of them. And there are private schools and universities worldwide that do good work."

"Ms. Madison, in most places the education serves the purpose of making the future citizens compliant with the way things are. After all, the main occupation, perhaps the only occupation of the human animal is the effort to maintain the status quo. Those who have can enjoy life – those who have nothing live in poverty. Education serves as a tool to accomplish this objective. But yes, you are pointing to the increased business factor of education."

"Mr. Sol, it is only about business. There are places where the young students receive loans they need to get the very expensive education. These loans never default, and the student is burdened by this debt for the remainder of his life and cannot pay it back because there are no well-paid jobs available. There are less and less jobs available everywhere. Similar to many other branches of organized human activity, education became a method to create a rift between people and the need to make money."

"This is very unfortunate. In light of such developments, what can the young expect?"

"This depends on where they live. If they live in a society capable of understanding the impact of technology and the needs for adjustment, the young generations will do fine. In all other cases. they will have only two options. To become a state servant who survives, or, regardless of education, be a working poor who is constantly harassed by increasing numbers of regulations!"

THE CABARET

February 21, 2018, New York City, USA
Mr. Wonderful – cabaret artist

"Mr. Wonderful, as the word goes, since 2008 you have made a lot of money with the same show. I got the flyer from it. Let me read it to you:

"Though there are at least 200 billion stars in our galaxy – the Milky Way, and there are at least 200 billion galaxies in the known universe, the only intelligent form of life can be found on our planet. The universe itself got created by a few very smart gentlemen who invented money. Ever since the dawn of time, money is being printed and used to create anything and everything we see and know about. There are no other creative powers in the universe, there is only money. So great is this power that by a single push of a keyboard button, the difference between starvation and wealth is felt all around our planet. Oh, how blessed we are, the ignorant, the poor, and the lazy sheep as we are called. We are blessed because we are privileged to live as long as those who command the only power in the universe, which is money of course, decide that we should live. And when everything is done, all that will be left is a lot of virtual money. There is a final prize for this game, and it is called the blackpot. He who manages to create absolutely endless debt that can never be repaid is rewarded with eternal life. He will live within a black hole in the middle of our galaxy, forever."

The cabaret artist could not stop laughing, and it took some time before he calmed down and was able to talk.

"Mr. Sol, this is an old flyer from 2008. We do not advertise our show anymore. The show is a major success. We only have one show at the end of every working day, and all the seats are sold well in advance."

"If I may ask, who are your guests?"

"Our guests are those who can afford our prices of course. A bottle of champagne starts at two thousand dollars. Almost all of our guests work in the nearby financial district; they are all people from the financial industry."

"What exactly is the content of your show? What is it all about?"

"Just like this old flyer tells, the show is about money. Money is the only thing that matters. Those who are in the position to create money out of nothing are the true masters of the universe. Everyone else should adore these people because of their power. Our show is full of humor, and our guests have a lot of fun, relaxation, and laughter during our show. It is a great success!"

"And what do you think about the show?"

"Before the show, I was homeless every now and then. Then I found a niche, which is this show. I make 7 digit earnings every year and I am doing fine. It is just business. I am an entertainer for those who appreciate and can afford my humor!"

"And what is the future of the young generations?"

"Future is a big maybe."

THE GOSSIP ECONOMY

February 22, 2018 – New York City, USA
Mr. Revere, independent economist

"Mr. Revere, the ways of our modern economy are often seen as illogical and out of control. The times when real work and product meant something seem to be forever behind us. Wild bets and speculation have taken over. What is your view?"

"Indeed, the old models are behind us. Perhaps they will return but right now, we live in what I sometimes call, the times of the gossip economy. Uncertainties of the markets, uncertainties about the value of the world currencies and obligations, and promises based on some future events, which may or may not happen, have led us into unchartered territories. What we are witnessing is a situation where information, false or true, has a direct impact upon the trustworthiness of the companies that are listed on the stock market, the trustworthiness of government bonds, and, in principle, the trustworthiness of anything has become questionable."

"It is an interesting definition, gossip, perhaps a rumor economy?"

"Yes, we have solid and stable companies that have proven business models and suffer from little if any systemic problems, and their value is downgraded because of the mood of the markets. When optimistic, the value goes up, when pessimistic the value goes down. The actual values of companies have, more often than not, nothing in common with the value of their stock as influenced by gossip. Development projects and new investments that make absolute business sense cannot acquire financing, but completely worthless venues that are indeed full of risk receive funding. We are seeing an erratic behavior pattern which is not based on due diligence, facts, and thorough wise analysis. In such an environment, completely healthy companies and business models can go under water in minimum time."

"But how did this happen? Is it just greed or is it something else?"

"Greed certainly plays a big role in this development. One has to understand that, for decades, great promises have been made, which were based on future events and calculations that turned out to be non-realistic. Promises of high returns on investment became more important than the question whether something is really doable. Slowly but surely, the lies became more and more present while the truth became something that cannot sell. It is a huge crisis of trustworthiness. Institutions and companies that were long considered to be trustworthy have lost their credibility while, at the same time, completely unproven sources of information gain instant, yet temporary credibility. Because of so many disappointments, people question anything and everything. Because of the lack of trustworthiness in the previously undisputed sources of information, gossip has moved into the domain previously held by trustworthiness. And as gossip goes, sometimes there is a degree of truth to it, but overall it is often nothing but wild speculation, misinterpretation, or even a deliberate lie."

"Mr. Revere, adults have a hard time understanding the times in which we live in. Adults, seasoned experts of various affairs, analysts, and otherwise highly trained and specialized people seem to have no real clue about what is coming next. Apart from defensive postures, most adults are really concerned and depressed. How can the young learn from our mistakes, and what should they introduce in their daily routines and thinking?"

"The young should be very careful not to be misled by gossip and rumors, just because the trustworthiness of the society is temporarily gone. They need to think!"

THE OBSOLETE HUMAN

February 24, 2018, Sedona, Arizona
Ms. Franklin, sociologist and blogger

"Ms. Franklin, Sedona is a really tranquil place with a great climate. I would expect more optimism coming from a writer who works from here. Your thoughts about the obsolescence of people are quite depressive and disturbing. Though we witness a major meltdown of workplaces in the Western world, is there no hope that the armies of the unemployed will find meaningful work?"

"Optimism is not about believing that wishful thinking has any chances of happening. Optimism is not about believing that some dreams will come true. It is motion pictures, computer games, and books where everything is possible. The righteous character eventually wins and justice is served. Optimism is actually about recognizing the true facts, the real situation, and, in accord with such real facts, a realistic solution is found. I am sorry that my observations and writings are seen as depressive, but there were many warnings on the walls – 20, 30 years ago, that told us well in advance that things would change in a direction that would be very disturbing, unless whole societies would adapt to new models of economy and society."

"You are talking about various books written in the 1970s and 1980s? During my travels, I am reading such books which were no best sellers, and I agree with you: The troubles of the moment have been predicted a long time ago."

"Mr. Sol, there are many factors one has to understand. The concept of eternal economic growth is obviously not possible with an ever rising population. To expect that ever increasing numbers of people will have all the items they would like to have is simply an illusion. The question of limited natural resources and the capability of speculators to increase prices of resources even when there is no shortage should not be overlooked. The modern technologies are also impacting our societies in ways that are realistically said, very different from what the masses need. At the beginning of the 21st century, many manufacturing and servicing tasks could be automated; the traditional human being as someone who does some work is becoming obsolete. Some say that already now, more than 60, perhaps 70%, of all the functions we see and use in our societies could be automated. People are increasingly becoming obsolete – that is a fact."

"Yes, this makes a lot of sense. But what will people do? We have to live somewhere, eat and drink something, wear some clothing, and otherwise people have many needs. How will people earn the money to pay for what they need if there is less and less work available?"

"Mr. Sol, the question should really be, how can increasing numbers of people, living in a monetary world, survive without money?"

"Exactly Ms. Franklin, what will become of all the unemployed, laid off, retired without pension, educated without prospect of employment, and all those who don't have any real skills and education? What is the future of our young generations and how much time will pass till a solution for this situation is found?"

"Well, I am certain that it will take decades before a new world has been established in which automation and people co-exist in ways that are satisfactory to all. In the years ahead, many people will simply have the fate of being obsolete and will die out. The young generations will have to be adaptive, wise, and disciplined in order to find ways not to become obsolete too soon. They need smart leadership!"

THE WEATHER

February 26, 2018, Desert View, Grand Canyon, Arizona
Mr. Adams, independent climatologist and writer

"Mr. Adams, thank you for taking the time to meet me. The scenery here is simply fascinating. It makes a person think about the world and his place in it quite differently than when confined to some urban area. My office informed you about the topic of my research. We thought that whatever we are going to create should not ignore the immense power of nature. You are an independent climatologist whose opinions are completely different than from what we hear from mainstream sources. I hope you can help me understand what is happening with the weather on our planet?"

"Thank you. People like me are predominantly being ignored because our views and conclusions are not producing money. The reason why I wanted to meet you here at the entrance of the Grand Canyon is to show you how unimportant our civilization is when compared to the forces of nature. Your office briefed me about your work, and I understand that you are trying to see into the future, is that correct?"

"Perhaps one can define my work like that. I like to think of my work as providing any number of likely scenarios to any question asked. But yes, we try to see the future and try to do it based on various patterns and cycles that have happened in the past."

"Then you could be a climatologist as well. For the past 30 years, a group of international climatologists have been exchanging data and experiences, and we all came to the conclusion, based on past evidence – some of which is actually recognized by modern science, that the weather on our planet behaves in accord with certain patterns and cycles of our planet, our sun, and possibly the universe in total."

"Mr. Adams, anyone older than 40 can remember that the weather is changing; the seasons are not what they used to be. Rains, draughts, storms, temperature fluctuations, and much more are occurring differently than what we considered to be normal. Our pollution of the environment is an undisputed fact, regardless of whether we talk about chemicals, radiation, carbon emissions, and waste of all sorts. Is the pollution of our planet influencing the weather or is there perhaps something else that makes the weather weird?"

"Pollution certainly has an impact on the climatic conditions. Pollution is man-made and visible. Therefore, mankind can be held accountable for pollution. The burning of fossil fuels is influencing the climate. Since there is an estimated worth of 25 to 30 trillion dollars of carbon fuels left, there will be no agreements among the powers-that-be to reduce the carbon emissions. One has to understand that this man-made problem, called global warming, is just a part of the problem when one thinks about the climate. When something is man-made then it has potential for taxation in the name of alleged solutions. You know, seeking business opportunities in everything."

"But you are not convinced that the weather is weird because of pollution only. You advocate something completely different?"

"Based on decades of research conducted by many educated people, based on various ice and soil samples, which with modern technological methods can be analyzed and reveal to us many details about our climate in the past, going back tens of thousands and even hundreds of thousands of years, we learned that our planet is continuously going through cycles. We are now at the end of the Holocene period, which lasts about twelve thousand years during which the climate is rather stable. This favored the development of the human species. The human civilization can do absolutely nothing about these cycles of our planet and celestial bodies."

"It makes a lot of sense, Mr. Adams. So, the weird weather we are experiencing around the planet is not something we can influence? Taxing people in the name of pollution will also not solve the problem? What is the most likely scenario for all of us when we think about the weather?"

"Mr. Sol, the scenario is simple. Our planet is considered to be 4.5 billion years old. That is a lot of time, a lot of history which we are just marginally starting to analyze. From available sources of information, we know that our planet, as well our sun, have cycles that bring different climatic models. Mankind has no solution for it. The actual reality is that humans with all their magic, called technology cannot do a thing about the influences of the celestial bodies, the sun, or the planets. The weather is weird, and the weather is changing, and the climate is changing in accord with proven cycles of nature. What we are about to experience in the years ahead is completely normal. The universe is constantly changing, so are the conditions of life on our planet."

"This also makes a lot of sense, Mr. Adams. If we think along these lines, meaning that the world is a continuous cycle of propaganda while the real forces at work are the forces of the universe, what should we pass on to the coming generations as real knowledge, as a real message about our climate and weather? What can the coming generations hope for? What is it that they should know?"

"The coming generations will live in a world that is changing. Most regions will experience severe changes of climate. Some regions will benefit from the coming changes. Some will no longer be suitable for human life as we know it. The problems created by us will not be solved because of the way the world works. There is no long-term strategy, morality, awareness, or even intent. The young generations will have to be able to adapt to the coming circumstances in order to survive!"

THE EPOCALYPSE

February 28, 2018, Portland, Oregon, USA
Mr. Washington, independent end-time theoretician and blogger

"Mr. Washington, Portland's Rose Garden is the right setting for our conversation. I can see Mt. Hood from here. Volcanoes have much more influence on the life of our planet than most people know about. Tell me about the dangers to our civilization."

"There are so many real dangers that we could talk about it for several days. What you don't see from the Rose Garden today are the other volcanoes in the northern direction, including Mt. St. Helens which exploded 38 years ago. For some time already, the volcanoes are quite active. The problem is that more than two thirds of our planet is covered by oceans, and much of the volcanic activity is not seen. Volcanoes are just one of our planet's tools when it is undergoing changes. Earthquakes can shatter our world in ways that are so dramatic that most people avoid the topic altogether. New diseases and also old diseases that have learned how to mutate based upon our influences are also very important. The changes in our magnetic poles, the magnetic shield of the planet that protects us from the harmful radiation of our sun, and many more things can bring up what I call an epocalypse, an ecological catastrophic event that wipes out the human race."

"Mr. Washington, at my institute we have comprehensive computer models that have shown us any range of scenarios and events that may occur at a certain time. Most of them are so devastating that no civilization can survive it. I have even seen scenarios where our planet loses its atmosphere and without air to breath we cannot survive. However, we live in hope and good will that such scenarios will not occur. What is your prime concern when you think about catastrophic events?"

"Oh, that question has a simple answer. In our world where profit is the only thing that matters, my concern is that some of the extinction-level-events the human species have prepared, will be triggered by some random event coming from nature."

"And what would that be?"

"The most dangerous scenarios deal with pandemics – the outbreak of lethal viruses that have mutated in nature or are a direct product of human research and development. Another very dangerous scenario is the question of radiation. As I stated already and many people know it, our planets magnetic shield greatly limits the lethal radiation of our sun. Same time, in the past 60 years, humanity has introduced hundreds of nuclear reactors which are very dangerous to anything living. Yes, nuclear reactors produce electricity for 50 years but the nuclear waste may last for a million years. Many things and many businesses introduced into our daily lives make business sense, but they do come at a price. Radiation is lethal as well as long-term. It affects everyone and everywhere. You cannot see it, just as you cannot see viruses. Both scenarios are utterly dangerous for all life. A third scenario comes from our sun which has massive solar eruptions happening all the time. It is just a question of time when a sufficiently massive solar eruption comes in our direction. Our magnetic field will not be able to protect us. Our power grids will take a serious hit and we will lose the supply of electricity upon which we depend so much."

"Makes sense, Mr. Washington. When thinking of young people, what should they be prepared for?"

"The young generations should learn the basics. How to make fire without matches is what counts. Learn something that you can use and apply in times of need!"

THE SUCCESSFUL TV SHOW

March 2, 2018, Honolulu, Hawaii, USA
Mr. Zwischenberg, the richest living producer of TV shows on our planet

"Mr. Zwischenberg, you are the most successful TV producer of our times. Be it talk-shows, reality-shows, or TV series, your name undersigns the most profitable and most viewed TV programming available today. I work on a product in which we use the input of free thinkers and doers of things. Would you please extend the courtesy and explain to me why your productions are so successful?"

"It did not come overnight. A part of the success story is, of course, that I am well connected and, thus, I do not need to chase the right people. I call them, they call me, and we focus on success. The other part of the success story is that I am producing any sort of TV programming which the vast majority of viewers actually want to see. I am not giving them something that will enhance their world-views, make them smarter or in any way, or influence their thinking. In most cases, I give them exactly what they want to see, something they can easily identify with and something they feel comfortable with. Additionally, I give the viewers whatever it is that they, the viewers, think is important. I give them entertainment tailored to their taste and needs. Think of me as the person that holds the mirror in which all these viewers get to see what they want to see. I tried to do it differently when I was younger, and I lost a lot of money on educational programming and all sorts of TV programming that would tell people about world affairs. I paid the price for thinking that I knew what the general audience wanted. I was wrong. Then, a few years of poverty taught me that the masses want what they want, and I am not the one who should question their needs and preferences. This is the secret of my success."

"Thank you Mr. Zwischenberg for your sincere answer. I often find myself thinking that the intellectual should influence the masses in ways that broaden the horizons. But I am confined to service knowledgeable people and companies, so I am not as well versed as you are when it comes to the general public. What does the general public really like to see and watch?"

"The general public likes to complain that they are misled and that someone somewhere is conspiring against them. When a group of carpenters find ways how to monopolize and divide the neighborhoods and raise the prices of their services, they keep quiet, spend the money, and feel good. When a group of bankers do the same, everyone complains. The truth is that nobody is really forcing anyone to do anything or to believe in anything. The general public seeks entertainment, fantasy, and humor in a format they understand. The masses desire to see people like themselves, having some fun or adventure, and nicely packaged with some good commercials along the way. Perhaps the easiest way of understanding it, is that they, themselves, want to be on TV! And this is what I am giving them; this is my magic!"

"And you went bankrupt with educational programming?"

"Oh yes, I did top quality educational programming, documentaries, art movies, and went bankrupt doing it. Then I lived several years as trash. I've been homeless, had alcohol and drug issues, my marriage fell apart, everything went down the drain. Then after several years had passed, an opportunity gave me the chance to change my life. I was strong and disciplined to accept the opportunity, not dwell on the past, and put all of my energy and talent to work. Perhaps the times of utter hardship and poverty did give me a qualitative edge. I am a compassionate person, and I understand the hardships and brutality to which many people are exposed. Perhaps this helps me in being successful in what I am doing?"
"And what is your next success? Are you working on something entirely new that can continue your path of success?"

"Sure. I am very thorough at what I do. I got a team of researchers and lawyers who look into all the possible opportunities. Right now, we are working on a new reality show, and I am sure it will be a global success.

My lawyers had to devote extra time finding out whether anyone may have legal right to sue us, but they did a good job, and we are starting with the new show very soon."

"What is this new show about?"

"I cannot tell you. But I will give you the name of it. It is called, 'The Retards.' I am certain that it will be the best reality show that I have ever produced!"

"This tells me about the state of affairs of modern television."

"I don't care, I personally never watch any television programming, not even my own shows. I watch documentaries and art movies; I don't need the box to entertain me, Mr. Sol."

"Very interesting. Mr. Zwischenberg, if you were to influence the young generations of today, in the times we live in, what would be your message to them?"

"They should have good filters when they watch any TV show. They can learn about the inclinations of the masses by watching television, but if they seek knowledge, real life experiences, and wisdom, then the young generations have to invest time reading the classics and earning the right to have someone mentor them about the many facets of life. They will not get that kind of knowledge from the box. They have to earn it!"

THE ILLUSION OF REVOLUTIONS

March 5, 2018, Sydney, Australia
Mrs. Parkes, international expert on revolutions and counter-insurgency

"Mrs. Parkes, we see ever more strife and protests occurring in countries that were considered immune to revolutions of any sorts. The mainstream media is not reporting the true numbers of people involved in these. How realistic are the claims made that anything can be changed by means of revolutions at the beginning of the 21st century?"

"I think it is completely unrealistic, especially when thinking of the Western world or the countries that can afford modern surveillance and military technology. What we see and will continue to see are organized attempts to reverse the tide of history. People in general have little if any wisdom. The world never went back to any previous state of affairs. The world is continuously and constantly changing. It is the natural order of things in the universe. Things change, people change, and the world is changing. To believe that, by means of protests and even revolutions, society can be brought to some previous levels of satisfaction and functioning shows us that those who believe in it are either provocateurs or are absolutely unrealistic. Societies that lived well above their means will never again live like that – at least for fifty years they will not. Most likely, they will never again walk the path in which the productive parts of society are milked dry so that the unproductive parts can live good lives. Therefore, the protests in the Western world are in principle, futile. They are an exhaust, vent, and they will not accomplish anything spectacular. At the best, some societies can collapse under the burden of debt and protests. When any society collapses it means chaos, population reduction, and immense suffering for many years to come."

"But the masses, or at least some people, do believe that revolutions are still possible and that they result in a new reality that is in favor of them. What do you think about that?"

"That is an absolute illusion. We live in a world of technological marvels that can easily offset any revolution at any given time. All the revolutions that are known to us were financed by someone behind the scenes, and they accomplished very little – if anything at all. In a revolutionary movement, it is always possible to pay off somebody, to infiltrate the core members, or simply coerce key members into betraying the doctrines of the revolution. Revolutions mean several decades of pain, misery, chaos, killing, and whatever nonsense that occurs during revolutionary times. And today, with a networked population who publish everything about themselves over the Internet, a revolution is easy to control and bring down. Additionally, any number of highly professional mercenaries can be brought anywhere in minimum time. Before you know it, these professionals finish their deed and are gone with the wind while the true revolutionaries are dead. Surveillance technologies and new inventions make it extremely hard for any revolution to succeed if the powers-that-be are against it."

"What should the young generations of today think about revolutions?"

"Revolution in today's time is only possible if a complete break-down of the society happens. When a society completely breaks down, it does not automatically mean that a better one will evolve out of the ashes. Young generations should be careful not to be misled by some revolutionary ideas, because things do not work out as they believe they do. Be careful what you wish!"

THE MAN-MACHINE SYMBIOSIS

March 7, 2018, Kansai Airport, Osaka, Japan
Mr. Isoroku Ohno, a guru of automation and robotic sciences

"Mr. Ohno, I have read many of your essays and wanted to ask you about your vision of the likely developments that address issues like artificial intelligence, robotics, and man-machine symbiosis. What can we expect in the coming decades?"

"We can expect many new developments, very much like those forecasted in some of the best science fiction novels of the 20th century. Technology is pursuing its own agenda and is developing too fast for most people to follow along. New developments and breakthroughs happen every few weeks. Huge amounts of money and many years of scientific work are at work. In principle, we need to understand where we are today before we think of tomorrow!"

"This makes sense. Where are we today?"

"The world is already divided among those who use technology on a daily basis, and those who have not yet started using it. Technology influences the way the users think and do things. Look at the widely available telecommunications gadgets. Instant communication is used very differently when looking the spectrum of usage. Some use it for irrelevant topics, while some users make the best out of it and increase their efficiency in ways unprecedented. One has to understand that many things are already possible, but they come at a price. Just like with anything else, it is the question of who can afford what. Perhaps the best sample case is the question of longevity. Life extension is already quite possible!"

"Yes, the majority live hard and, apart from dreams that do not come true, their real life circumstances are such that they see no reason to prolong their life. Longevity is really something for those who can afford it."

"You see, we are narrowing down to the real questions when we ask ourselves about what is possible. I like to think of it as what is actually affordable. Within the next 20 or so years, it is quite possible that some people will have their lifespan extended either by modern medicine or by means of entering into a symbiosis with machines and robots. The question really is, who can afford it? We made some calculations and came to some interesting conclusions. There are no real guarantees against common accidents. Accidents happen and are a major contributor to the death of people. Anyone who wishes to extend their life for several decades will have to spend several tens of millions of today's dollars in order to succeed. The eventual format in which such life extensions are possible can be much varied. My personal opinion is that the 21st century will present many different, often very strange forms of altered human beings. Some will look similar to us while some may look like some monstrous combination of a half human, half robot-like creature. Depending upon the preferences of the paying clients, it is conceivable that some will opt to live consciously without a body, their mind being part of a computer storage device or perhaps a cloud on the Internet. There are countless options for life extension."

"What should the young generations be ready to deal with, Mr. Ohno?"

"The young generations of the 21st century will be confronted with numerous difficulties as well as opportunities that have not been encountered by anyone in our known history. The only way to deal with it is with an open-mind. I think that open minded people will find ways to make their own lives worth living!"

THE FUTURE OF THE INTERNET

March 9, 2018, Shanghai, China
Mr. Xen, Independent Internet Security Advisor

"Mr. Xen, I decided to ask you about the future of the Internet as the majority of the Chinese are dependent upon it to a large extent. The Internet started as a US military project and has become the new world where anything is possible. It is the battleground for the hearts and minds of the users. There is increasing debate, around the world, whether or not the Internet should be regulated and controlled more than it already is. What do you think about these matters?"

"Yes, a lot of nonsense is happening on the Internet. Those interested in crime will use it to advance their nefarious agendas. Those interested in learning will use it for increasing knowledge and skills. If the Internet would be more controlled, without the opportunity for accessing it anonymously, like spreading rumors or providing alternative opinions and news, it may well look very different from what we have today. This can only make sense if a global consensus is reached and all the world powers agree that the Internet should become a highly regulated affair. I do not think that the world of today is as unified in order to accomplish any significant agreement of this sort."

"Mr. Xen, the Internet is already quite controlled regardless of what people think."

"It is to an extent, and it differs from country to country. The Internet as it is today has many benefits in terms of providing first class information to various security agencies of the world. People are providing tons of information about what they think, what they fear, what they do, with whom they do it, and where they do it. Profiling of Internet users saves lots of time and money when compared to actually profiling people in the old fashioned ways. You know, to shadow someone and to inspect someone's home without the person knowing it requires both skilled manpower as well as resources. If one uses the Internet for such purposes, one can gather much more information in much less time. Then when you have profiled the potential suspects you can devote traditional manpower and methods to that individual or group. I think that the question, whether the Internet should be or should not be more strictly controlled, is something which will be decided between the various powers that have interest in this topic and the decision will be made based on which solution provides most benefits to them. Some features of the Internet will undoubtedly become more controlled in the near future. I think that the benefit of the users openly providing information about their own lives offsets any benefits a firmly regulated Internet has to offer."

"In your opinion, what is the main danger of the Internet?"

"The Internet connects people at the speed of light in ways that they would never connect without it. It has both positive and negative potentials, especially in the field of spreading ideas and experiences. He who could control the whole of the Internet and all of its content could actually create a new 'reality' and a new version of history."

"Mr. Xen, since the young generations are so Internet savvy and used to it, what is the main concern you have about their Internet usage?"

"The Internet may become unavailable at any time, and unless the users have memorized valuable knowledge and practiced skills with their own hands, they may face serious difficulties adapting to a world without the Internet."

THE MANUFACTURER

March 12, 2018, Guangzhou, China
Mr. Lu, manufacturing plant designer

"Mr. Lu, you are one of the best regarded manufacturing plant designers, and your services are sold years in advance. What is the trend in manufacturing? The majority of governments and economists talk about the creation of jobs, and the need to create ever more jobs in order to balance the national budgets and provide people with sources of incomes. What does your experience tell us?"

"Mr. Sol, both governments and economists live in their own world and think about the world of manufacturing in terms of the 19th century. One cannot blame them, because most bureaucrats and economists have no working experience in the manufacturing sector. Therefore, they tend to see the world as they would like to see it develop. The real trends are, of course, quite different. We are now in the 4th decade of global outsourcing of jobs, especially manufacturing jobs. It all made sense as long as there were people willing to work for less and less wages, but this also brought various side-effects and implications that one could not have predicted a few decades ago. Nowadays, any manufacturer who mastered the art of organizing qualitative manufacturing knows that if you want to remain in the business, you have to automate as much of everything you can. He who is not utilizing modern technology is surely going to lose his market share and will eventually have to downsize or declare bankruptcy. The trend is automation: The introduction of automated processes steered by custom-made software that run all sorts of robots."

"Mr. Lu, how will this affect labor markets? Aren't the low wage countries immune to automation?"

"The automation process is a must. Especially in low wage countries many have learned that the low wages have to rise in time. Low wage labor also has significant impact on the long term quality of the manufactured product. We know that unless one runs a planned economy, it is the market demand that decides what will be manufactured in accord with the demand of paying customers. Planned economies have the tendency to fail at some point in time. Market demand means that the demand for products fluctuates; there are times when there is less demand, and no manufacturer can afford to keep all of his employees in such times. Rehiring employees is a process, and more often than not, the market demand fluctuates at a pace which is incompatible with strategies for laying-off and rehiring workers. The only solution is to invest in full automation because it is more durable, is more flexible, and can cope with the demands of the markets more easily. From the perspective of any manufacturer, automation is here to stay. The effect, this will have on the labor market, is simple: People will have to find some other occupation. This is something the majority of governments and economists do not wish to understand."

"If I may ask, where are your clients located? Who is ordering your services?"

"I receive orders from China as well as from North America and Europe."

"Given the trend of automation in manufacturing, what should the young generations consider, how should they prepare for the time when there will be less and less labor demand?"

"I am not an expert on issues of human resources. I cannot answer this question. They need help from their respectful governments in order to prepare for the coming times which are not so far away!"

THE COMPUTER SIMULATION

March 14, 2018, Singapore
Ms. Wise, computer programmer and blogger

"Ms. Wise, you are a highly regarded computer simulations expert. You also contributed to several bestselling books, some of which are already in their fifth edition. What is the influence of computer simulations on the general public?"

"It is absolute and much better than television ever was because it enables the person to be a part of the development. The actual sales figures tell us that most people prefer simple games with lots of action and simulations of destruction. It already did the basic training for the first generation of remote warriors – you know, young soldiers who operates lethal drones around the globe."

"Is this the only influence that the computer simulations propagate?"

"No. There are many sorts of computer simulations. For example, we have very complex simulations that put the player into the commanding seat of a whole world of civilizational advances and mega events. But these simulations are for the thinkers. They are not so much suited for the muscle type of people."

"I know what you are talking about. I have played advanced simulations for 25 years since they first became publicly available. It is amazing how there are some eternal rules of the human species. I tried many times to win by means of science and culture, only just to be destroyed by a heavily armed, militaristic computer opponent."

"Yes, people have serious shortcomings that are eternal and technology cannot change it. The potential of computer simulations is immense because it influences the way coming generations see the world. The question, of course, is of the guidance that we, the older generations, provide to the coming ones – what is it that we wish to leave as our cumulative heritage?"

"What do you mean?"

"I think about education. Much can be done in better ways by using computer simulations – in terms of actually learning, in terms of experiencing, and in terms of understanding whatever is being simulated, or, better said, trained. The problem remains to be a question of values, ethics, and morals."

"Where does it lead?"

"It leads into the direction of acceptance. Accepting whatever is computer simulated. This virtual reality is actually forming the reality of people. The personal computer is a much more efficient tool for forging public opinion and public acceptance than radio and television combined. It depends upon the programming. I repeat, the masses think that we create a virtual reality. Some do. As a matter of fact, we program the virtual reality to be in line with what we want the users to perceive as the common reality. For this reason, the personal involvement of the user, which is made possible through personal computing and which is exceeding any involvement the viewer ever had with television, is the key to understanding the power of computer simulations. The user thinks and feels that he actually has the real experience. He is aware that it is simulated but if it is trustworthy enough then the user accepts this virtual reality as the only real reality."

"So it is about programming?"

"Yes. Programming is very important. In principle, any individual can program himself in many different ways. The problem is that most people do not know how to program themselves. Most believe that the way they are, often ignorant, is just the way it should be. Many do not even understand the true potential of the mind. Perhaps the simplest explanation is that essentially everything happens within our mind. Yes, we have a body and that body may hurt. But the pain is registered in our mind. Unless we have a mind, we are nothing but a piece of walking meat. It is the mind that matters. Remember the saying – mind over matter?"

"Could we teach people how to program themselves?"

"There are many different techniques and teachings that deal with programming throughout the ages. The tools are different, but it is the same topic. The majority are not really interested in it because it is serious effort. It is much simpler to allow oneself to be programmed by someone else. Till the advent of computer simulations the best way to program people was by means of television. Technologies and the tools change but it is all programming!"

"What about the coming generations, will they continue to allow to be programmed or will they decide to program themselves?"

"In the majority of cases, the young have no choice. They are born into the world, and they do not understand it. By the time they start to understand the subtle details, they are already programmed and conditioned. Perhaps the only open question is whether there will be more competing sources of programming in the future allowing the option to choose one's own reprogramming."

THE HUMAN RESOURCE

March 16, 2018, Pune, India
Mr. Ambedkar, entrepreneur and human resource specialist

"Mr. Ambedkar, you are the CEO of one of the fastest growing information technology companies. What is the secret of your success?"

"Apart from the fact that we offer qualitative services at lower costs than many of our competitors, I find that our cumulative investment into our employees is the main reason for our continuous success. I view the human resources of our company as being our key competitive advantage. We invest in the process of education of our future employees, and we offer them employment security."

"This reminds me of my own life. My employer have invested in my education and provided me with job security. In return, I am giving the best of what I can give to them. It sounds like a proper strategy to me."

"Mr. Sol, your Institute is known to be the leader in their line of business. My company intends to be in business in decades from now, based on the principles of investing into our human resources. We believe that content and happy employees have a definitive competitive edge over the employees of other competitors. You see, most companies follow the principle of purchasing complete people. They do not invest in people, they just purchase them. This leads to a business culture filled with fluctuations. Money alone is not the only ingredient that assures that an employee is loyal and dedicated to his work and the company. We like to think of ourselves as long-term partners, we create long-term relationships. It is successful."

"And how does this principle influence your relationship to your customers?"

"It is an extension. Since we are a company composed of content people who know that they have a long-term interest to function together as a productive and qualitative team or unit, we extend the same to our customers. Our customers learn very quickly that we are dedicated, available, and interested not only when there is work that can be invoiced, but also in times when our clients need assistance in their own business. Contrary to many others, we will not make overnight changes to our staff that benefits a client of ours. We allow our clients to meet and talk not only with our sales people, but also with the team that will be dedicated to the needs of our client. We do everything we can to bond with our client. There are cases where our clients experience fluctuations in their workforce, because someone has been offered a better paid position and leaves his post. In such cases, it is our team that assures continuity, because we can substitute for the fluctuations happening at the side of our client. This often leads to additional business for our company for the reason that some clients choose to outsource more of their work to us. We believe in the benefits of long-term qualitative and trustworthy relationships. We do not lose clients. Our way of doing business assures that by word of mouth, new clients come to us. We do not invest much money into advertising at all. Our work is our best advertisement. In time, this track record develops into a powerful sales tool."

"Mr. Ambedkar, we live in dynamic times and many say that the global economy is undergoing major, tectonic changes. What should the young generations look for when thinking about education, employment and team-work?"

"They should think long-term. Not in terms of only striving to become government employees. Young people should seek and offer long-term commitments, dedication, and loyalty in the private sector as well."

THE START-UP ECONOMY

March 19, 2018, Jerusalem, Israel
Mr. Moshe Rosenbaum, start-up expert and blogger

"Mr. Rosenbaum, you have a magnificent track-record of both forming as well assisting successful business start-ups and, therefore, I wish to learn more about this buzzword which we hear more and more as a successful economic model."

"Please call me Moshe. Yes I been lucky with many start-ups and after a while when you learn how to do it then there is even more success!"

"Thank you Moshe, you can call me by my first name as well. It is Victor! As my office relayed to you, my interest lies in identifying new ways to help the young generations master the many challenges in life – economy and prosperity are definitively some of the key challenges. Can you provide me with a bit more insights as to why start-ups really make sense and whether it is just a temporary hype or a trend that will stay with us for a longer period of time?"

"Victor, I understand that you are in the ideation phase which is expected to result in something new, a new service or a new product. Thus what you do will eventually become a start-up. If what you create is interesting and if you have access to the right people with additional skills, knowledge, and access to capital then whatever you envision might indeed become a successful business model. It might!"

"Moshe, you summarized it properly. Access to additional expertise and direct access to interested capital are quite essential factors. How many start-ups actually succeed?"

"Generally speaking it is like everything else, the grand majority of attempts end up as failures. Only a small fraction of the start-ups actually

146

succeed, but if one knows how to do it and chooses proper fields of interest than the odds are much better. I have reached a level of sophistication whereby every third start-up I help create is a success, and these are excellent odds!"

"In which fields of interest is success possible?"

"They are always niches where there is still room to create something. There will always be significant problems regardless of whether or not some new product or service offers actual solutions in a particular field. For example, in the case where grants are used to develop something new, the main problem becomes insignificant adoption of the services. One of the reasons for such a situation is the absence of the budget for marketing, which is often overlooked. I focus on artificial intelligence, 3D printing, and advanced security solutions. Earlier I focused on energy and health related products. It is the niche that matters!"

"Moshe, how do you envision the future of the young people, and how can they perhaps apply the start-up model in order to achieve something?"

"Start-ups as a model are indeed a buzzword. It takes a lot of expertise to create a successful start-up and theoretical knowledge alone does not suffice. In order for something to succeed there are many important variables to consider, one of which is actual practical experience. Going through failures gives one great practical experience. Failures are part of life. In my opinion, the young generations have to accept that failure is part of life and that practical knowledge is often much more important than theoretical information. Experience is most important, thus, it all goes back to some form of cooperation among different generations!"

THE BUG CONVERSATION

21 March 2018, the Institute, Switzerland
Mr. Max's office

"Welcome home, Sol. Six continents in minimum time, what is your impression?"

"It is complex. I had many excellent meetings with interesting thinkers and doers of things. I also had sufficient time to look around and observe people in various countries, follow up with local mainstream media, and I am again realizing that the economy remains to be of major concern to the masses. Some places everyone is very optimistic while other places pessimism and end-time thinking rule the day. No matter what many people say, it remains to be a big planet with very diverse cultures. I am still uncertain about what we should create for our client!"

"I've been busy too. Since the last time we met and my travel to South East Asia, I was able to acquire several new contracts for the Institute. One of which is a major success. An Asian corporation involved in social services asked me to help them out, urgently. I want you to see how I found a solution to their problem. Namely, they were unsure whether there is something fishy in a potential project they got themselves involved with. A developing country's leadership approached them with an ambitious project of introducing basic social care in a country of several tens of millions of people. Everything looked well, for example the conditions of public to private partnership looked good, but our client still felt insecure. So I called some old friends and asked them for a favor. It is amazing what modern technology can do. How much do you know about bugs?"

"You mean bugs as insects?"
"Actually yes, Sol. Bugs as insects and bugs as eavesdropping devices. Have a seat and look at the footage on the big screen."

The 60-inch screen showed footage, obviously taken from a surveillance drone. A five vehicle convoy entered a luxury resort in some unspecified country. The footage changed from bird's-eye view to a rather imperfect video stream when Mr. Max pressed the pause button on the remote control.

"What you have seen is the moment when the leaders of the unspecified developing country arrived at their secure resort, after they had two days of negotiations with our client. These are smart people, so they never talk much over the phone and my friends tell me that nobody was able to infiltrate the resort. This time more modern technology got used. The sound is good, but the video feed is imperfect, yet is good enough to get the needed information. Watch and listen carefully!"

The video feed of rather low quality went on for several minutes, and the conversation, between what obviously would be cabinet ministers meeting with their president, was quite relaxed before the crucial part of the conversation was recorded.

"Mr. President, we have successfully completed our negotiations with the Asians. There are still some minor issues, but we believe that we have obtained our main objective. They will invest 10 billion dollars into the development of our basic national health care system as a public-private partnership model. This allows us to roll out our original plan. The Asians will pay for the visible part of our services, and we will start collecting the moneys from our people, quite soon."

The camera moved leftwards capturing an elderly gentleman whom everyone addressed as Mr. President.

"My ministers did good work. If everything goes as planned, we shall within six months collect more than four billion dollars from our people in the name of advanced payment of mandatory basic health insurance. The elections are in nine months from now, and we all know that we will accomplish what we wanted during this term in office. We will phase out of the country, the five of us, leave the new government with a major success story at their hands, and till they realize that, apart from the Asian commitment, there is no money in the account of the special fund for the development of the basic national health care system, we will be far away, filthy rich, and secure."

Mr. Max pressed the stop button on the remote control.

"You see, this was a perfect deal that went wrong. The locals were able to convince their citizens, the parliament and even an international corporation of the merit of introducing a basic national health care system in a country that never had something like it. Yet it is nothing but an elaborate fraud. Had I not had some old contacts and had science not invented new types of surveillance gear, we would have not known that it is a fraud. Our client is now very satisfied and happy."

"Max, yes, it is amazing. We should find out who the manufacturer of the artificial bugs is and buy shares of the company. Guess they have these surveillance bugs in all shapes and sizes?"

"Surveillance bugs are designed and manufactured to match the actual climate and insect species of any world region. Amazing what miniaturization can offer, you think it is a fly or mosquito, yet it is a sophisticated flying surveillance device. But there are other events that may interest you. Professor Wunderberg will visit us in June. I am sure that he might help you figure out what it is that we seek for our client."

"That is great news; I could surely use his thoughts in this project. I will now meet the project team and exchange notes with them. In a few days, I will depart to various European cities to meet more free thinkers and learn from them."

"You may as well make a videoconference call with our client in the coming days."

Sol spent the remainder of the day with the project team envisioning the product that Mr. Goodwill had asked for. This process was still at an early stage. Sol ordered a global opinion poll to be carried out in the coming months. He wanted to receive as much potential feedback from the masses in order to understand what it is that they would need in the near future.

THE VIDEO CONFERENCE CALL

March 22, 2018, the Institute, Switzerland

"Mr. Goodwill, we are making breakthroughs in our conception process. As of now, we need an additional round of consultations and fine tuning with outside sources and we will have to wait for the results of the global opinion poll we ordered. I am confident that we are moving into the right direction, so I wanted to brief you and ask you two questions."

"Excellent Sol, you are all doing good work. Let me hear the questions."

"Sir, if we create something that can really help the young generations to understand the world they are born into and how to make the best out of their individual situations, the question remains whether they would actually use it. We cannot guarantee that. Are you willing to take the risk of launching a global service that may take time till it shows its fruitage?"

"Sol, the answer is – yes. If I can provide a tool which could make the young generations smarter, I will back it up with my wealth and other assets. I like it!"

"Second question. There is sufficient pessimism around us. Many think that the world is coming to an end or that the future will be very ugly. Do you still want us to create a solution for such end-day scenarios too?"

"The answer is again – yes. I will back a product that can equalize the devastating effects of any major catastrophic event happening to all of us. Just keep with the schedule we agreed to. I will be at the Institute in about nine months from now. And I expect that by then you have conceived the product and have all the blueprints."

DEMOCRATORSHIP

March 28, 2018, Frankfurt am Main, Germany
Mrs. Schmidt, social worker and blogger

Sol opted to meet a few more thinkers in Europe since they were nearby and perhaps acquire a few more insights that could be helpful in the ideation process of the product, which would enter the finishing phase by September of 2018. Meeting Mrs. Schmidt at a cafe overlooking the Main River beneath the skyscrapers of the financial center of Germany, popularly called Mainhattan, felt like a proper setting for the conversation that followed.

"Mrs. Schmidt, you have coined the term 'democratorship' as being the most likely form of governance in the 21st century in all the regions of our world where democracy is being practiced. To me, this sounds like a fusion between democracy and dictatorship. What is it that you actually mean with this term?"

"I agree that the term is a bit of a provocative nature. I did use two words to create it, and democracy is, of course, one of them. The other word used is not dictatorship. The other word is stewardship. My thoughts originate from three decades of work as a social worker, and my additional experiences in various non-governmental organizations involved in the development of a civil society."

"So it is stewardship which you use as an ingredient for it?"

"Yes. We are all born into a world that is as it is. In this world there are people and institutions that are who they are and do what they do. As individuals we cannot really shape this world. What we can and should do is find ways of managing it."

"I get it. In a democratic world one should think about how to manage all issues confronted by the society. One should see to be a good steward of the society. Is that your main thought, Mrs. Schmidt?"

"It gets a bit more complex than that, Mr. Sol. I devoted no time to the territories where principally brutal and outright feudal regimes determine the fate of the society. I looked into the world of democracies and what it really means in the early 21st century. Fact is that we already live in a virtual democracy, which in most cases cannot pay for all the promises made by its leaderships in the past. Neither can these democracies really provide everything what the population wants or deems as necessary. Even better, most of these established democracies have no solutions to anything except to create various spins and float disinformation. We have to recognize the real situation and provide alternatives on all levels of the society in order to assure a sustainable model that can help us make the best out of the available circumstances in the decades ahead of us. This led me to the concept of virtual democracy and virtual citizenship out of which it became clear to me that we need to think about stewardship over the democracy we were born into!"

"Virtual democracy, virtual citizenship, life is not a virtual affair or is it?"

"It all depends upon what any individual thinks or believes that life is. The real impact of one person – one vote is indeed, virtual. All the advocated rights, freedom of speech, human rights, and social rights are also relative. These are great ideas and concepts but in a material world in which we live, one has to question how much of anything is sustainable, whether it is affordable and whether it makes sense when observed from the viewpoint of costs and benefits. While we all wish to believe that certain rights we were born with are forever given, we also realize that much of it cannot be afforded. Affording it leads us to the potential collapse of our societies!"
"Mrs. Schmidt, how do you see the life of a virtual citizen living in a virtual democracy or even better said, what is the possible future for the

citizens of democracies in the coming future based upon a system of democratorship?"

"We already have a system in place which functions along the lines of a class society in which those who are unproductive are given a life standard that exceeds the life standard of productive people in other parts of the world. This system is being misused and costs too much. Unless this system, which went bankrupt many decades ago and the endless creation of debt is changed, all these societies will collapse and nobody will have anything but chaos. In this chaos, the ones that will be hurt the most are the ones that are loudest when it comes to ignoring the problems of our societies. Those who contribute little or nothing misinterpret the real problem. If I am giving you everything you have because you are not capable of doing it yourself, then it is not you who will tell me how much I should give. It is me who tells you how much I can afford to give to you. The German welfare system is based on productivity and availability of export markets. Perhaps Germany can maintain such a welfare state?"

"Yes, the national budgets are non-balanced since at least the early 1970s. People do not understand that there is no such thing as an endless free lunch. What we witness is the time in which the old ways are fading away and some new ones have to be introduced if we want to continue to live in a civilized society. But what is your recipe Mrs. Schmidt, what is your vision?"

"As a social worker I learned that there is only as much one can do for the endless numbers of people who did not find their productive slot in society. It is good that there is a safety net that helps catch those people who are falling, but the system can no longer be misused and taken for granted. I do have a vision, Mr. Sol."

"Please tell me more about your vision, Mrs. Schmidt."

"If our societies wish to continue maintaining organized and civilized benefits, we will have to adjust the benefits of the masses and find ways of dealing with the unproductive segments of society. Those who are unproductive will remain to be so for a long time to come. There has to be some level of minimum and affordable life content that is provided to the unproductive segments of the society. A person sleeps for six to ten hours per day. What to do with the rest of the day? We need to think about the present and future young generations of basically unproductive and, thus, virtual citizens. Together with a group of associates we came up with the model of a sample case virtual citizen. We call it the Helmut Model. I guess had we been in the United States, we would call it the Joe Model."

"Tell me about the Helmut Model."

"Helmut is born into an unproductive family of welfare recipients. He is assured from birth to receive 20 m^2 of free housing, a certain amount of kWh of electricity per day, a certain amount of m^3 of water per month, a certain amount of calories per day, has free flat rate Internet access, receives one free computer and one television set every three years, has a sufficient but limited number of free software downloads per year, and he has the right for a certain number of free medical services per life-time. If Helmut wants to receive any sort of education that exceeds the basic skills of commanding a language and basic mathematics, he can do so using online learning which is free. If Helmut wants to become a productive citizen and change his life, he can check and compete with everyone else using the free databases that announce and provide productive employment opportunities. In times of election, he can vote via the Internet and he has freedom of speech as long his spoken and written thoughts are not addressing topics about which he knows nothing about."

"So what does Helmut do every day with what he has? I presume you have lots of experience on this topic. As a social worker you are exposed to hundreds if not thousands of destinies of people who are unproductive."

"We consider that a high percentage of the Helmut type of people will play computer games most of the time. The computer games are big consumers of time. Before you know it, the day or the night is over and you are tired and wish to sleep. Your ego is quite satisfied, because in the virtual world of computer games, you can be almost anything you wish to be. A billionaire businessman, a successful manager, a celebrity, a mighty general, a secret agent, a race car champion, and you can even extend your lifetime to cover thousands of years during which you take charge of a nation or the whole planet. Your ego is satisfied, and it doesn't matter that in the world outside of the computer game, you are an unproductive person. As long you are immersed in the computer games, you are whatever you want to be. You can cheat your results, or you can play games at higher realism settings. You have endless options, and you lose the concept of time. You have a roof over your head, food in your stomach, and your life has content that can be changed in accord with your free will and interest. Helmut is docile, not interested in other things because he knows that the world outside the computer is not favorable to him because he is not competitive enough. On the other hand, if Helmut wants to become a productive citizen, he can do so. All the tools are given to him, free of charge. Helmut can never say that he had no option or choices. Helmut is taken care of and in return he is compliant with the real reality of the society!"

"And the productive citizens in such a society of the near future, what do they do?"

"The productive citizens take care that everything functions and that the budgets are balanced. They are the stewards of the world. This is democratorship!"

COMMON SENSE

March 30, 2018, Budapest, Hungary
Mr. Zentai, politician and blogger

The Fisherman's Bastion on the west side of the Danube River built in the late 19th century is a beautiful terrace with seven towers designed in neo-Gothic and neo-Romanesque style. The views of the Danube River, the Margaret Island and the east parts of the city are very inspiring. This was the setting chosen by the Hungarian host who was about to meet Sol and talk about the self-interest of nations.

"Mr. Zentai, you are a seasoned master of politics and a popular blogger. The main thought you are writing about is the need for the reestablishment of national interests and the pursuit of, as you call them, common sense agendas in order for the societies to survive and thrive. Are we not living in the times of centralization on a global level? Don't you think that you are advertising an outdated model?"

"Mr. Sol, when we talk about outdated models, we might want to think about what the real model is all about. Listen to a story I was told when I was a boy. It is a story about alleged events hundreds of years ago."

"Tell me the story."

"It happens in the feudal past. One day the tax collectors came empty handed from the serf settlements and reported to their master that something very strange was going on. Wherever they went, the tax collectors found that all the serfs, the adults and children, had hung themselves from trees. A massive suicide campaign was occurring and the tax collectors could not perform!"

"That is indeed the nightmare of every tax collector. Please continue."

"Next morning, the feudal lord rode on his horse to the nearest town to meet the religious authorities. As he entered their comfortable office, he started to shout. Did we not have a firm agreement? It is my responsibility to keep the serfs preoccupied and poor while your responsibility is to keep them ignorant! Unless we do something urgently, there will be nobody left to work. Unless we do something now, you and I will have to work!"

"I like this one. What happened next?"

"Next morning an organized effort started throughout all the lands controlled by the religious authorities and the feudal lords. Based on the trustworthiness the serfs had towards the religious leaders, they were made aware that they cannot escape their destiny. Yes, the life of the serf is hard. But to think, to believe that by committing suicide a serf can escape his destiny is an illusion. From that day on, the serfs were made to believe that if they choose to end their miserable lives a much harsher penalty awaits them. The surfs started to believe that any personal choice to end misery leads to eternal damnation, eternal servitude, and hell. Ever since, the serfs did not commit massive suicides. They accepted their fate as they were told by the feudal lords and the religious authorities. What is the lesson of this old story?"

"To me it sounds as a beautiful sample case of applied propaganda."

"Mr. Sol, look at the bridges over the Danube River. On paper, these bridges can belong to anyone, including someone on the other side of our planet. In the day to day physical reality, these bridges have no function except for the masses who use them on a daily basis. The owners can claim that they purchased these bridges and they want to see profits made on their investment. The owners can lobby local laws and introduce bridge crossing fees. The owners can employ armed guards that will control these bridges. The owners can lobby additional local laws that forbid the building of new bridges or any sort of transport across the river. But, at the end of the day, these bridges have only as much value as the local population assigns to them. Nobody can assure nor force, in the long-term, that they will use these foreign owned bridges. The owners may try to do so, but in the end, it is the people who live in this city who will determine the fate of these bridges. Hungary and the rest of the former Eastern Bloc countries in Europe have been brought to its knees. Massive unemployment, huge disparity in purchasing power, declining life span, declining quality and availability of basic civilizational advances and social services, all of this is reaching a boiling point. The owners can do whatever they want, but they cannot convince the local populations that the path we have taken is a good path. We witness the rampant re-introduction of the lowest of feudal practices for now more than two decades. Nobody cares about some great ideas that may happen when all of us are dead. What we need to think about is how to live now and how to organize our local societies along lines that makes sense to the local societies. This can only be done if one follows an isolationist path. We have to think of ourselves, first!"

"Mr. Zentai, what lies ahead for the young generations if they wish to live and thrive?"

"The young generations will have to accept the reality that without real work, without real effort, and some personal sacrifices the future will look grim. They have to accept that they will have to be hard working people, and that it will take quite some time for the results of their labor to be positively felt in the immediate societies where they live and work. They have to focus on their local societies and not be misled by any agendas that do nothing for the local community."

LIVE NOW AND PAY TOMORROW (OR NEVER)

April 2, 2018, London, United Kingdom
Mrs. Beckett, investment banker and writer

"Mrs. Beckett, you have written many interesting articles for the mainstream media about the financial flows of our time. My office explained to you what our interest is. We create products for specific clients. Our groundwork is almost done and after many, many smart and knowledgeable thinkers with whom I have connected and talked to, I wanted to meet you because of the fact that wherever one goes, looking into any problem, it turns out that the real problem is money, the lack of money, mismanagement of money, and so on. What is your opinion about the current economic and financial crisis?"

"Mr. Sol, I suppose we will not talk about all the fine details of money because we could talk for weeks and still be missing some important elements. What we are witnessing is the demise of many national economies at a scale not seen before. Perhaps this is the topic you wish to talk about?"

"Mrs. Beckett, it seems that such failed national economies multiply in scores?"

"Mr. Sol, this brings us back to the question of how money works. For almost five hundred years, we have lived in a world of banking that is based on the fractional reserve principle. The Internet is full of explanations, thus, I need not elaborate on this. What we witness today is a serious problem that was known that could happen, and it is not being addressed properly. When you purchased your ticket to London, you used money and not chocolate, did you? Day to day transactions between people cannot function on barter principles only. Money is the solution. Thinking of money as a means of investment, it is understandable that money is an entity that looks for ways to multiply. Money will go to those places, to those people, to those projects that have the best chance of the money invested being multiplied. Why would money go to someone who will simply waste it? The allocation of money, where it is spent even at loss because it is needed for a society to function, is the responsibility of national governments. What we are witnessing is the unaffordability of national welfare systems. Many have adapted to a permanent lifestyle of living and spending now yet paying for it tomorrow. Too many people and leaderships believed that there might be ways not to pay the accumulated debt at all. This is now coming to an end and, of course, it has dramatic and harsh consequences. The most vivid sample case from history is the fall of the Roman Empire, since it was the Roman Empire that minted money which was accepted. After this disappeared, it took Europe some thousand years till new money that would be accepted by all got introduced. Hopefully we will find a solution to the current problem and avoid the repetition of history, the demise into lawlessness and chaos."

"And what is the end-result, Mrs. Beckett? What is the short-term future? How can all these societies come back to their feet? How can people avoid utter poverty?"

"Mr. Sol, I am not a soothsayer. I wish I could answer such a complex question. If one thinks along the line of how money works the answer is quite simple. Things will change to the better only for those people, those groups of people, those societies, and those leaderships who re-discover that the best way to assure prosperity is to be productive. Individuals who are productive can be found in many places, but they are burdened with an unproductive surrounding. I am afraid that there is no solution in less than two generations time. Of course, even in the worst off societies that once enjoyed solid life standards there will be a fixed percentage of people who are productive in ways that are unproductive from the perspective of money!"

"I am unsure that I understand what you mean?"
"All the economies, where the only secure paycheck goes to government employees and where nepotism or political suitability decide everything,

will maintain a small but fixed percentage of allegedly productive and paid people. Such economies will bleed the population dry. The state will find any sort of taxes and regulations to take as much as they can from the population. This can go on for years and perhaps decades. I am sorry for the really productive people in such economies, but I hope that this tiny minority of thinkers and doers of things will find ways to emigrate somewhere else where the environment is positive towards productivity."

"And what about austerity measures that are so popular right now, Mrs. Beckett?"

"Mr. Sol, this is nonsense. It is one thing to downsize the spending habits of people, to streamline the national administrations and otherwise optimize the spending of money. But uncontrolled austerity is actually the wrong thing to do. You do not get better quality of work and services for less money. People who have no money spend no money, and the tax incomes of the national states get smaller day after day. Austerity as it is practiced right now is no solution to the problem at all. It is part of the problem and deliberately so!"

"This makes sense. What should I tell my children about their future?"

"Raise your children to be productive people. Adaptable to the circumstances, accepting the real realities of the world they live in. Money likes productivity. Money does not support long-term non-sustainable economic models. If your children learn to be productive and organized, they will have a future worth mentioning."

THE BENEFITS OF AUTOMATION

April 4, 2018, Brussels, Belgium
Mrs. Maxine, automation specialist and blogger

"Mrs. Maxine, your work about the impact of automation on the Western societies is not much known to the public. You are focusing on Europe and provide very optimistic views of the not so distant future. What are the benefits of automation?"

"Mr. Sol, I am focusing exclusively on Europe. We hear and read a lot about the need to employ people from other continents because the population of Europe is growing old. This is a major oxymoron that tells us about 19th century thinking that ignores the benefits of automation and creates a false impression about the aging issue. Namely, Europe does not need any new labor force coming to Europe because the continent already has tens of millions of unemployed. First of all we need to understand that especially in line with all the agendas about conserving natural resources, ecology, and the reduction of the human footprint, Europe is in an excellent position to balance itself and take care of itself by means of using the opportunities at hand. In the modern world, human numbers are not telling of their capabilities. Those who still believe that power and strength comes from hundreds of millions of people constantly, ignore that it are not the numbers but the organizational forms as well the skills of any society that make a difference. The aging process in Europe is opening up new workplaces not only for classic workers but also for supervisors and technicians of automated processes that will take care of the elderly. Lower demographic figures mean that in the times we live in, the continents that have fewer mouths to feed are gaining in competitiveness. It does not matter nor is it something to worry about if Europe has 300 million instead of 500 million people it has today. It is a great opportunity to streamline the societies of Europe!"
"Less is more?"

"Absolutely it is. Europe has to undergo a balancing act which will include all facets of the society. We have armies of unemployed and many will never find work unless they are retrained. Therefore, we retrain them in accord with a concept of a productive society. Who cares whether someone has a degree or skills in something that is no longer needed? The world is changing and people have to change with it. The question is, where do I find work and what sort of work is it that can feed me? Europe has excellent opportunities in the years ahead. Automation of many daily processes of the society will allow the functioning of the society. Same time, automation provides for new job opportunities. The high levels of current knowledge and scientific capabilities in Europe have to be steered into the direction of producing quality items that cannot be matched by other continents. The still present infrastructure of Europe allows for good transportation and quality life conditions of its population and, at the same time, a proper setting for high quality manufacturing of all sorts. Europe needs to re-define itself, balance, re-adjust, and within less than two decades it can reach a sustainable continental model. Only when this is achieved should it devote time and resources to other continents. Not before!"

"And what stops Europe from doing this rebalancing and readjustment act?"

"The bureaucracies will have to adjust to the real affordable levels of administration. After all, administration already is highly automated by means of information technology and communications. There is no need for huge armies of administrators, and no matter how hard it sounds to them, the bureaucracies will have to balance their budgets just as every other facet of the European societies has to do. There has to be a real master plan which is not a brain-cloud of some sorts, but a master plan that puts Europe first. Everything else will be dealt with later."
"This tells me that there is a lot of work ahead of Europe which many would like to avoid. Do you really see it happening during our lifetimes?"
"Different continents have different roles to play and are facing different circumstances. There are plans to introduce modern production facilities

that will employ millions of robots and this is happening on the continent
which has the most numerous of all populations, Asia. If Asia is going into
that direction why would Europe avoid regaining competitive advantages
it always had?"

"Mrs. Maxime, you know that there are agendas that seek ways to further
the sheer numbers of people. There are societies that are diligently
doubling their populations every twenty years or so."

"Yes, there are many different societies and each and every one of them
has its own responsibility. If they pursue a path that is not sustainable and
they cannot afford it, then it is their problem."

"Mr. Maxime, let us imagine that the powers that rule over Europe decide
to take the necessary steps and readjust the European economies and
societies, introduce automation that compensates for a declining
population and otherwise, do what it takes to balance a whole continent.
What would such a new Europe look like?"

"It would be a continent where the levels of unemployment could be
financed because nobody could enjoy unemployment benefits forever. The
continent would have 40% less population, would consume much less
food, water, and other natural resources, the products made in Europe
would be of exceptionally high quality and durability, and the pursuit of
profits would move into some completely new fields of activity and
interest. Such a Europe could exercise its fair share of influence and
interact with other continents because it would be a balanced continent. It
would not be weak; it would not be too strong. Such a continent, such
Europe could pursue many important objectives which we miss today.
Such a Europe could actively pursue, develop, and field new cultural,
technological, and social achievements. It could even reinstate firm values
and morality. Eventually, such a Europe could then also help others deal
and overcome with whatever problems others face."

"What about the world? How do you see our planet, the human species, and the co-existence of the many different societies on our planet in the future?"

"You mean from the perspective of automation?"

"Yes, from the perspective of automation. What sort of a world will it be when one thinks about young people and their role and fate in it?"

"Mr. Sol, it was always much easier and simpler to think about the solutions for the world than to pay attention to the actual day to day situations and problems of an individual or a society. We have six inhabited continents and each of them has its benefits and shortcomings. One day in an unspecified future, these six continents will act together, yet each continent will remain its specifics with regard to the human element and the climate. The young of today or tomorrow will have the same role our generation had when we were young and others before us."

"Which is?"

"Well, they are born into a world which is governed by adults. The sooner the young learn about the ways the human world functions, the better it is for the young generations themselves. It is all about the learning curve and gaining wisdom!"

THE LOST GENERATIONS

April 9, 2018, Paris, France
Ms. Germaine, philosopher and blogger

To many people who have seen it, Paris is the most beautiful metropolis. The last of the many interviews, talks, and consultations, Sol had in 2018 happened in the Louvre Museum of Paris, amid exceptional works of art.

"Ms. Germaine, you are a popular philosopher with a broad audience. Your blog is exceptionally well-visited and many people look to you for guidance. You believe that the young generations are actually lost ones?"

"Yes, we are witnessing at least one lost generation not only in the Europe but in North America as well. I have carefully studied the fate and performance of the youth in the transitional economies of East Europe after the fall of the Berlin Wall in 1989. What I learned was that the majority, perhaps 90 to 95% of the young people could not find reasonable ways to accomplish anything because of the transition of the affected economies. Unless the young came from a well-connected family or unless they found ways to move to some other national economy where they could work and get paid, the majority of them achieved nothing. They made no money, lived with their parents, had diplomas which had very little real value, and they did not find their place under the sun. These are the lost generations of the transitional economies, and the same is happening in the West today!"

"Ms. Germaine, I learned a lot about optimism in Africa, Asia, and Latin America. Does this mean that the losses of the Western generations will be to the benefit of generations elsewhere?"

"Not necessarily, Mr. Sol. These are very different worlds. The Western one is definitively experiencing a crisis. The rest is to a high degree always living in a crisis and much of the new optimism found there is an illusion based on some relatively shallow assumptions. We have huge regions that are burdened with hierarchical models that have never brought prosperity to the majority. This has not changed. The high birth rates in the rest of the world are offsetting all the visible improvements of these societies. In economic terms, the world is interconnected. Once the Western markets stop purchasing cheap goods manufactured in what basically are slave driven regions, then these regions will face severe unemployment problems. This will affect the regions of the world that depend upon their exports of raw materials and they will too face real problems. It is a chain-reaction which will take some time but it is inevitable. Our human universe is seeking a new formula and has not yet found it. Perhaps a new Cold War needs to be introduced, again splitting the world into two blocks, in order to reorganize global economies."

"You and many others talk about a crisis which is not exclusively of economic origin?"

"Mr. Sol, our societies are going through a major crisis of values. This has been elaborated on by many smart minds in the past decades. Look at our societies at the beginning of the 21st century. What do we see to be the predominant topics and patterns of behavior?"

"Well, it is different than it was fifty years ago. Consumerism always existed and people were never really friendly if you ask me, Ms. Germaine. But the times are such that one has hard times to find decency, due diligence, trustworthiness, personal integrity, long-term commitments, and much more!"

"Mr. Sol, our crisis goes much deeper than the visible problems of debt and excessive consumerism. People became very vicious. People enjoy mocking others, feeding off of other people's problems and tragedies. People became rampant liars who will cheat and betray anything and everyone in order to achieve whatever personal goals. The personal goals are, in most cases, not attainable which makes people even more aggressive. There is lack of thoroughness, lack of zeal, lack of moral values, and much more. At the same moment, there is an exponential rise of ego-trips by the masses, self-gratification, and lots, lots of vanity."

"I agree with you Ms. Germaine. But how will this end?"

"It does not end. There are no real beginnings or endings. There is a continuous flow of changes and transitions from one state into another. Right now, we experience a crisis of the times of transition. After a while, this transition will be over. The world will again enter a period where everything seems to be properly functioning before another change and another transition creates another crisis."

"What should the lost generations of today do with their lives?"

"They haven't got many choices. The lost generations will have to do what they can to survive and adapt to the circumstances. They will have to find ways to enjoy what is affordable and available to them. They have to come to terms with this situation!"

After the Louvre meeting, Sol returned to the Institute and joined the rest of the team working on Mr. Goodwill's product.

THE CREATIVE MOMENT

June 11, 2018, the Institute, Switzerland

One morning, Sol's first mentor showed up at the Institute. After meeting
Mr. Max and looking into the most recent algorithms the Institute was
using, Professor Wunderberg joined the Sol family for a private dinner in
their residence. Sol's wife Virginia was especially pleased to have an
opportunity to meet one of her husband's early mentors. The evening was
young, and the professor had an announcement to make.

"I am pleased to have been a part of your early life and to have had the
privilege to help you find a productive and fulfilling path in your life. At
the age of 80, I have decided to retire from all affairs and spend the
remaining years at a beautiful tropical island observe the world events
unfold and only communicate with people by e-mail. I leave tomorrow
morning and have no intentions of flying on a plane after this final flight. I
am happy to see you with your family. An intact family is one of the
greatest achievements a man can wish for in his life time."

"Professor, my husband mentions you on a weekly basis. Sometimes I was
jealous of all the attention he would devote to your e-mails. When you two
would meet at some seminar, he would talk about you for days. I wish to
thank you for the positive influence you had on him. Without you, we
would have never happened. I am very pleased to finally meet you. What
is this place where you are retiring to?"

"Virginia, my wife died and my daughters have their own lives. The world
is in no need of an old and boring academic, and I am also tired of world
affairs. I found a retirement home, which is rather luxurious, and I can
afford it. It's in the Caribbean, has excellent medical care and on-site
amenities. I will have a small beach house and have already shipped all the
gadgets and things I need. Arthritis is bothering me and the warm climate

should alleviate some of the pain. There I will have the best of everything available to me."

Sol realized that he might not meet his mentor again and that made him sad.

"Professor, you were the first mentor in life. I had no clue of what I should do. I only had this tremendous appetite for knowledge and lots of ideals. The decision to use my grandparent's modest inheritance to finance the start of my academic education would have been a mistake had you not helped me with the scholarship and your recommendation to work for the Institute. You and Mr. Max enabled me to live a fulfilled and productive life. I am eternally grateful to you."

"Thank you Sol. I can no longer call you an apprentice. You are a young master in his own right. You make me proud and I wish I could have helped more young people in finding their place under the sun. You know, most people do not have the luck to find a true mentor during their lifetime. I extended to you the same that I received from my mentor. I hope you will do the same when your time comes. This is how we influence the world in positive ways. We pass our knowledge from generation to generation."

As the professor ended his sentence, Sol dropped his cup of coffee and sat speechless, almost in a state of shock. Virginia rushed to collect the broken pieces of the cup before the children would accidentally step on them. Sol stood up and started to walk around the living room drawing designs with his hands. The professor stood up and walked towards Sol asking him:

"What is wrong? Did I say something that has upset you? Are you feeling well?"

"To the contrary professor, to the contrary, this is possibly the most creative moment in my life. You see, I got a new assignment which is very ambitious but pretty vague and I could not really see the solution. An old client of ours tasked us to create a product that would help the young generation experience the joy of living. The client does not want just another product that promises something. He wants the real deal. And you just told me what it is that we have to develop. Can you please summarize what our relationship is, what you did for me, and who did the same for you?"

The professor smiled and took the stance of a scholar addressing a big audience.

"There is this great Hindu saying, 'When the pupil is ready, the teacher appears.' When I was a young man living in Europe there was optimism around, but it was a time of hardship and austerity. My chances to reach any fulfillment and happiness were marginal. Then a person whom my father knew advised me to emigrate to the US and explained me how to do it and what to seek. I followed his advice and it brought me happiness in life. This person was a sort of a mentor to me. When I met him again years later, I asked him how could I repay him. He replied that I should extend the same to other people. I followed this throughout my professional life. This is why I opted for the less paid job as a professor teaching at universities. I gave you some attention, helped you understand a few things, opened up a contact that could help you develop further, and that was it. The idea is to pass the wisdom of humanity from one generation to another. By doing it, we are influencing the world in positive ways. We are changing the world to become a better place for all."

Sol returned to his sofa and snapped with his right hand fingers.

"You have just identified what the product that we should develop is. We have to find a way to increase the number of mentors available to young people without restrictions and limitations of social status. What we need to develop for our client is a variation of what the Institute does for its clients. It has to be a system which will pass the experience, knowledge, and, above all, the wisdom of the experienced generations to the coming ones."

Virginia applauded, recognizing the uniqueness of this creative moment.

"Now I know why you two have a special relationship. Bravo! This is productive brainstorming. I don't think any of you realizes the potential of this moment. Young people are completely confused. Everything they have been told is falling into pieces. We have perhaps the best educated generation on both sides of the Atlantic that is facing the destiny of lost generations, no job, no income, nothing. I think about our children, and I do not see any meaningful future for them unless we as parents can assure sufficient wealth, which will pay for their basic life expenses once they grow up. The young generation is burdened with accumulated problems of their ancestors and nothing constructive is being done to help them master the immense challenges that lie ahead of them. The current problems are so immense that adult people find little if any solutions. How can one expect the young to find any solutions if we do not help them in that process? I think that you have just identified a solution that may indeed be of real help to the young people!"

The professor enjoyed Virginia's compliments and asked for more coffee and cake.

"Perhaps technology can be used to make people wiser. Not all but sufficient numbers of people wish to become wiser but do not know how. There has always been this tendency to simplify things and believe in promises. It is easier to believe than to actually do something. I would have failed as a mentor if your husband would have been ignorant. After all, I just helped him understand and identify the moment and move in a direction, which made most sense based upon his talents and social status. Had he been from a rich background I would have advised him to become a state employee in his native country. I think he would have fared well in diplomacy too, but because his family had no particular social status I knew that he would never reach the potential he had. The only way for

174

him to grow and become productive was to work in the private sector. But had your husband not worked, learned, and had he not invested into himself, he would have failed."

The professor made a pause and asked for even more coffee before he continued.

"As a mentor you cannot guarantee that anyone will actually follow your council. But I do agree with you Virginia, our civilization has already failed and betrayed the current young generation as well the coming ones. The future may well be a dystopian world in which brains are not needed, and the people are empty shells that live as drugged slaves. The alternative is to have a generation that is aware of the complex challenges, capable of becoming wiser in much less time than any of the known past 300 generations. This is the only hope for humanity if we wish to see a flourishing, creative and in all aspects a civilization worth mentioning. People need to get wiser and more responsible, and they need to get there in an accelerated fashion. If you have a client that wants what he said, to help people experience the joy of living, then you have the chance of your lifetime, Sol. I know you always wished to be part of something that may help improve life on Earth. I was like you when I was young. Maybe I can help in this project?"

"I thought you are retiring to a remote Island from where you will watch the world enter its demise? I did not get the impression that you intend to remain active."

"Sol, my body has to retire. I have no intentions of becoming a cyborg of some sort. My mind is not retiring. As I told you, I have already shipped all the equipment I need. My intent is to live for the rest of my life as a brain on the Internet. I will communicate with selected people, why not? I need no money, what I do need is some form of preoccupation that makes sense to me. If you define this system properly, maybe I can participate. I can provide my humble knowledge for free. A lot of my colleagues have retired and would gladly extend their knowledge to others. I am sure that I can convince them to join a project that helps the human race. The problem is that the young often do not want to listen, and the other problem is that it makes no sense to consult someone who is not yet ready. Remember the Hindu saying – 'When the pupil is ready, the teacher will appear.' If you and your team can figure out a system that makes sense, I guarantee you that I can mobilize at least a hundred wise people to be the first mentors who participate."

The next day, Sol's family took the professor to the airport. Old friends also came by and said goodbye, perhaps for the last time in person. They knew that as long as their brains were functioning and could access the Internet, they would stay together and share many moments of creativeness and friendship.

The input of the free thinkers, the immense database of the Institute, and much more, all contributed to the ideation process of the future product the client wished to offer to the world. But in real terms, it was the creative moment experienced with Professor Wunderberg that gave the whole effort the right direction.

THE GLOBAL OPINION POLL

August 17, 2018, the Institute, Switzerland

The results of the global opinion poll ordered by Sol came in. It was analyzed and an executive summary was formulated. Mr. Max and Sol were going through the results while sitting on a bench in the shade observing the cows at the Institute's pasture.

The opinion poll was conducted in 120 countries on six continents. Three age groups (16 to 25, 35 to 45, and 65 to 75 years of age) were asked the same set of questions. In total, 3,334,108 people provided their opinion without any preference for race, place of residence, gender, and religious affiliations.

The opinion poll gave two major conclusions:

-       As the people reach more actual life experience (age), they become aware of their own mistakes, and how their own mistakes influenced their lives in ways that, no matter how much one tried, could not be corrected. Life does not give a second chance, or, when it does, people often do not recognize it. The older and wiser the masses get, they understand that there is nobody to blame for their individual mistakes. Most mistakes result from a thorough lack of understanding of the human universe and the world.

-       The people are less and less interested in any sort of politics. They accept the hierarchical models of society, as long these provide a standard of living for them and fair justice. They are able and willing to accept any hierarchical model and any leadership that can actually deliver such standards and conditions of life for them

The opinion poll summarized the reasons why personal mistakes are made:

-        There was a lack of understanding of the situation
-        There was no understanding of the consequences of personal decisions
-        There was no available trustworthy person to ask for advice when needed
-        Naivety and wishful thinking influenced the decision making process
-        Life experience was inadequate to make any reasonably smart decision
-        Absence of specific knowledge pertinent to the problem
-        Personal ignorance and impulsive actions contributed

Focusing on the age group of 16 to 25 years of age, the opinion poll concluded:

-        They do not know whom to trust (trustworthiness)
-        They do not know whom to ask (lack of proper contacts)
-        They do not know how to ask (question of interface)

The same age group (16 to 25) provided additional input that can be summarized as:

-        The human interface may not be the best way of acquiring council and advice because many have the tendency to judge others wrongly – by age, by outer appearance, and other basically irrelevant issues.
-        They are already conditioned in ways that prefer to interact with computers, databases and networks instead with fellow people.

-        They are increasingly driven by short term motives of instant success, self-gratification, idealistic thinking, belief that they know it better, and that there must be certain shortcuts that can be taken in order to achieve personal accomplishments in minimum time.
Based on the comprehensive data received from the global opinion poll, the elders of the Institute and the supercomputer that run various

predictive software, game theory, and forecasting of behavior and social engineering patterns came to the following recommendation:

-       "Computer interface" as a trustworthy source of information that contains knowledge and wisdom would be welcomed. Because they are already embedded in the world of computing, computer simulations, handheld gadgets, and the Internet, the time is already right for:

-       "The Optimism Database" which the users could consult on almost any issue and situation. The off the shelf computing power, storage capacities and software already allow for such a database be brought to operational status in minimum time. Algorithms need to be developed, but these can already make use of other complex systems in existence today.

-       "The personal avatar mentor," who is available to every user, learns about the individual user and follows up on the user's circumstances and situations. Such a digital mentor could eventually be made available at a time when the whole system is automated.

-       "The trustworthy interface" would mean that the users (the people) interact with a computer system that helps them understand the risks and helps them understand the realistic chances of success or failure of almost any situation. Such interaction between the human being and an "all knowing computer" would be preferred over the interaction between the classic relationships of mano a mano, or, person to person.

WRAPPING IT UP

The remainder of the year 2018 was an extremely busy one at the Institute. Sol asked for additional manpower, and Mr. Max gave him anything and everything Sol needed. The technical staff was testing various electronic gadgets. The computer hardware staff was determining the computer power needed for the Optimism Database. The software team and the mathematicians were involved in mock-up programming, and the development of a basic testing platform that could present the envisaged system to the customer. Various free-lancers and outside associates were called in to develop the proper formats of the system such that everyone can understand it. Economists were playing with business plans and different roll-out scenarios. Lawyers looked into numerous laws in different territories of the world to identify the proper legal format for the envisaged service.

Mr. Max was meeting various major names from different industries and checking who might want to join the project in order to make the project possible. Sol was in a hyperactive creative mode of thinking and working. Together with Mr. Max, he would go to the mountains and nearby rivers to field test various versions of the product. They were concerned with the possibility that the world would experience a major cataclysmic event. If that happened, the software would still need to work. All in all, everything was on schedule as the client expected.

CHAPTER 4: OPTIMISM

(2018)

Fortune truly helps those who are of good judgment.
Euripides

THE TIMES OF CHANGE

December 21, 2018, the Institute, Switzerland

Mr. Goodwill arrived in the morning hours and settled in the Institute's VIP villa. At 1400 hours, Goodwill, Max, seven of the Institute's wise sages, and Sol met at the restaurant. The client addressed everyone present.

"Ladies and gentlemen, I am pleased that you kept to the agreed schedule. You are a trusted and reliable partner. The world of man is like an Ostrich. Humanity has its head buried in sand, not wishing to see, hear, or talk about fundamental problems. It is like a mountain whose foundations cannot hold its own weight. The bottom disappears, and in time the whole mountain collapses within itself. More than before, we will need good judgment to deal with the increasing number of situations that will challenge our societies. I hope that the product the Institute created will be of assistance in this demanding process that is ahead of us!"

Mr. Max smiled and raised a glass of red wine.

"Dear Mr. Goodwill, it is said – by their fruits you shall know them. Your fruitage is one of a real philanthropist. We thank you for your attention, trust, and business."

Everyone raised their glass, honoring a man to whom humanity and our planet are more important than personal ego.

THE PRESENTATION

December 21, 2018, the Institute's Agora

Sol opted for the presentation to be held using the rotating globes and the narrative computer voice. The Agora darkened and both globes rotated slowly, their color being light blue. Sol walked towards the rotating globes, turned towards the audience and addressed the client.

"Mr. Goodwill, I wish to personally thank you for this assignment. After twelve months of work, everyone involved came to the conclusion that this is the most beautiful, most inspiring, and most idealistic project we ever did. It is a chance to use the creative power of human minds in order to create something that may have the potential to make this world a better place for our children. We have created two different products in accord with your wishes. The second product will be presented in Mr. Max's office, while the primary product will be presented by our supercomputer because, as you will understand, it is the right setting for what we have created. Both globes will show video footage and computer animations that relate to the content of the presentation. You may wish to know that the artificial intelligence (AI) of our super computer is exceedingly advanced. We created the product ourselves and compared it with what the AI recommended, and the result was quite astonishing. We learned that in the world of non-detached analysis, looking at the problems from a non-personal perspective, the recommendations made by us and the computer are very similar. Therefore, the product is absolutely feasible. What you are about to see is workable and can be fielded within minimum time. It is not fiction. Computer, please start the Optimism presentation!"

Both globes started to rotate. Each one presented different pictures from all walks of life. Then the rotation stopped, both globes turned off their color, and the Agora was completely dark when the pleasant computer voice addressed the audience.

"Right now, every single second, almost two people die on this planet. One has to think about all the knowledge, all the experiences and skills that are in most cases completely lost. Only in rare cases did people achieve a real transfer of knowledge and much more important, wisdom, to others. The valuable wisdom is massively lost. Apart from very confined numbers of individuals, wisdom is not taught, it is not passed from one generation to another. Some wisdom is preserved and available to the people by means of proverbs, such as – what goes around, comes around – and thousands of others. Interestingly, throughout the 4,000 plus nations, the proverbs are quite similar and contain the wisdom of at least 300 generations of human beings that have existed. The other source of wisdom that is still available is contained in classical works of literature. There are also prophecies, religious books, and various others texts that are available but the content is often burdened with deliberate propaganda. In general, people are not acting in an intelligent manner. They have a solid potential to combine the natural resources of the planet with the creative potential of the mind, in order to co-create a world which would be progressive and creative. By the early 21st century, it is evident that selfishness, vanity, fraud, embezzlement, theft, pride, wastefulness, procrastination, greed, irresponsibility and self-destructiveness are on the rise. The billions of people who have lived did not find a way to extend their wisdom to the coming generations. It is a very unfortunate situation. Unless something is done that will raise awareness of this destructive pattern, there are no reasons to believe in a positive outcome."

The Agora lit up in pleasant green colors. Both globes started to rotate and portrayed the pictures of newborn babies.

"Right now, the estimate is that every single second, more than four people are born into this world. One has to think about the absolute inexperience of them, who are born into a world they do not understand. If humanity is to reach its true creative potential we need three ingredients: knowledge, wisdom, and ethics."

Knowledge

Is to be aware and command information, skills, facts, blueprints, descriptions, and the way how something is made possible, how it functions, how it can be built, maintained, or operated. Knowledge is earned through education and experiences and can be of theoretical or of a practical nature. Knowledge is not wisdom. The computer voice elaborated:

"Knowledge has never before been available as it is now. Humanity has huge pools of knowledge. Our creation is, therefore, not focused on knowledge because it is already widely available. Increasing numbers people access all sorts of knowledge even in remote regardless of social status and climatic conditions. This trend is increasing as telecommunications and information technology are spreading on all six inhabited continents of the world. Even the basic smartphone makes knowledge available in vast quantities and can be accessed regardless of social status, gender, race, or religion. Seekers of knowledge can access it in previously unprecedented ways. A planet inhabited with increasing numbers of knowledgeable people has better chances to survive and thrive. However, knowledge alone is not enough."

The globes stopped again and portrayed the definition of wisdom:

Wisdom

Is the ability to understand how the world, people, situations, events, things, thoughts, ideas, problems, and many more function. Wisdom is the art of how knowledge is used or not (lack of wisdom). Wisdom is the key ingredient of judgment. Judgment is the evaluation of all variables needed in order to make a decision. A decision is the selection, the choice between any numbers of possible actions taken. Wisdom requires the control of emotions, and the ability to analyze and observe anything from a non-personal perspective. Wisdom includes knowledge, principles, reasoning, and experience. Wisdom leads to good judgment which leads to good results and outcomes. It is gained by a lengthy process of experiencing different situations. The best way for someone to gain wisdom is to have the privilege of the attention and dedication of a seasoned and experienced mentor who already reached some level of wisdom. Wisdom also addresses the questions of ethics.

"Wisdom is much harder to access than knowledge. It takes a lifetime to reach some levels of wisdom, and it comes at the expense of making many errors in judgment till some wisdom is gained. Errors in judgment always come at a cost. People have the tendency to make errors. Some of these errors have devastating effect for the society as a whole. Analyzing the available technologies and the habits of those who use modern technologies in ever increasing ways, we have identified an interesting niche. It is already possible to accelerate the process of gaining wisdom for all those who wish to become wise. We do not know how many will seek to become wiser, but just as knowledge is broadly available we consider that wisdom should be broadly available as well. Right now, humanity lacks sufficient quantities of wisdom. We are herewith presenting our identified product!"

The Agora changed its background light into light blue, the color of a clear sky while the globes presented the definition and basic diagram of the product.

The Optimism Database

The Optimism Database is comprised of a central computer and a data storage system. The system processes the interaction between mentors and users. With time, this will become automated, namely the cumulative experience is learned by the AI, which will in time provide direct answers and suggestions to the users.

All the situations processed are stored, and the AI learns in due process and increases the amount of wisdom that is made available to the users in an automated fashion. The more the Optimism Database is being used, the better it becomes. It can be available by means of personal computers, tablets, and smartphones. It can use cloud technology. The Optimism Database is software, which can use any type of present and future hardware. This provides it with longevity.

"The Optimism Database will offer ever increasing wisdom about ever increasing numbers of situations. It is an expanding, open-minded platform which will accommodate the interests and needs of users. It will help transfer wisdom from those who already reached some level of wisdom to those who need wisdom in order to master whatever situations they are facing. It can also remind the users of certain master objectives, master agendas, and master principles that affect the whole of human species and the planet itself. Here is a simplistic overview of the different fields of interest that the Optimism Database will cover. Please note that almost any number of situations and fields of interest and activity can be addressed. For example here is a basic listing of some of the fields that the Optimism Database will cover:

- Personal relationships
- Social relationships
- Business relationships
- Education counseling
- Career counseling
- Legal counseling
- Consumer counseling
- Financial counseling
- Friendships
- Fraud protection
- Business ethics
- Morality and ethics
- Principles
- Productivity
- Creativity
- Responsibility

-      Parenthood
-      Ecological awareness
-      Situational awareness
-      Understanding the trends
-      Love
-      Self-programming

"The Optimism Database will include ethical principles defined by the providers."

The globes started to rotate faster, while showing various potentialities that a user might ask for guidance about. Animations of young people using notebooks, netbooks, desktop computers, tablets, and smartphones while communicating with the mentors – facilitated by the Optimism Database – accelerated and accelerated. At the same time, the computer's voice slowed down.

"The product can be available to anyone who has access to the Internet. There is no discrimination and all users have equal rights accessing the Optimism Database. For the start, there are 108 available mentors who will provide the nucleus of wisdom. The number of available mentors will increase, and the system has no limitations with regard to the number of mentors or users that can use the system."

Then the rotations of the globes slowed down. The left globe transformed into the image of a wise person representing the older generations. The right one transformed into the image of a young person representing the coming generations. Both images extended their hand to each other while the computer's voice summarized.

"The Optimism Database is a tool that will allow for a previously unseen transfer of wisdom from those who have obtained it to those who need it. Like a parent telling the child that a wise person learns from the mistakes of others, the Optimism Database provides a realistic chance for the coming generations and the society as a whole to avoid expensive and often fatal mistakes that are made because of shortsightedness, ignorance, impulsiveness, and a general lack of proper judgment."

The presentation ended. Mr. Goodwill and Sol exited the Agora and walked through the Institute's underground corridors to the computer workshop area where the product would be further explained.

What Should I Do?

The computer workshop area was filled with all sorts of computer equipment. Across a ten meter mahogany desk were personal computers, notebooks, netbooks of different sorts, half a dozen of tablets, and a dozen of smartphones all running the demo of the Optimism Database. Walking around the desk and reviewing the different gadgets, Mr. Goodwill started to understand the practical aspects of the product.

"Sol, all of this equipment is running the same application, the Optimism Database?"

"Yes Mr. Goodwill, we spend a lot of time creating a mock-up Optimism Database and tested different delivery channels in order to make sure that the product can be fielded with today's technologies. A supercomputer runs all the information and processes any question which is then directed to the proper mentor. We have 108 mentors available online who can provide their wisdom, and the supercomputer takes care that the proper mentor is contacted by the user. It is match-making at its finest. At the same time, the computer is learning from the interactions between the mentors and the users."

Mr. Goodwill looked at all the different computer equipment, picked one smartphone, and walked to the nearby sofa to take a seat.

"Sol, let's simplify. How does one use the database, and are there any differences in the service whether it is used on one or the other platform?

Sol took a notebook and seated himself next to Mr. Goodwill.

"We all know of situations in life where we ask ourselves, what should we do? Well, the concept is that any time a person has doubts about a situation in life and feels or thinks that he might not know what to do, the user of the Optimism Database can simply ask for council, ask for advice. And this is done through a graphical interface that is user friendly. It starts with logging in to the Optimism Database and then either typing the topic, the question, or using the provided menu in order to get connected to the most appropriate available mentor who may provide reasonable council. It is very similar to using Internet search engines. At the beginning, every interaction will be between the user and the mentor. Later, as the database is being used and as it accumulates wisdom, more and more will be answered in an automated fashion by the supercomputer. The different equipment will have some different options of course. A smartphone or a tablet may not offer the full range of potential services as a notebook, netbook, or that of a personal computer. In addition, we consider that an additional option would be to provide a symbol, icon-based communication, something like a cartoon. This could have the potential to bridge the language gaps as well to accommodate those who are illiterate."

"What is the full range of potential services of the Optimism Database, Sol?"

"Starting with a quad core processor and sufficient RAM, we foresee the possibility to have a stand-alone application reside on sufficiently powerful personal gadgets. This would be the individual, customized, personal avatar mentor that would serve the user much better than a simple app for a smartphone. Using today's technology smartphones and tablets, we foresee for the time being a simplistic online communication between the user and the mentors made available through the database. In the case of sufficiently powerful computers, the users could purchase their own program which updates with the database in similar ways to that of an Internet security program that frequently updates its repertoire of viruses, spyware, and malware. On a sufficiently powerful gadget, the users would have their personal, customized mentor. It could be used in offline mode under certain circumstances but its full functionality requires online communication with the database."

"Sol, what is a personal avatar mentor?"

"This will be a very comprehensive product. In principle, it is a miniaturized version of the database. It runs on supercomputers because it has to. The personal avatar mentor would be a standalone application which, once installed on a computer, would customize itself to the exact needs of the user who purchased it. It would be the personal mentor containing the wisdom of countless of wise people. The reason why one needs customization is because everyone is different. Therefore, every person deserves a personal mentor. In our case, an avatar mentor. One can have any face or many faces act as the visible mentor on one's computer display. I repeat, this is a customized product and the buyer has to pay for it. The better the processing power of a computer, the more complex analysis can be provided. It learns, it customizes, and becomes your personal crystal ball. Something similar to what we as the Institute do for our clients. It can analyze the complete situation of a person, based on endless parameters and provide the very best of council on all types of affairs. It updates online with the Optimism Database in order to become smarter and wiser. Alternatively, the personal avatar mentor can be made available as cloud computing and then you need less powerful personal hardware. In any case, because it is custom designed for an individual, this product comes at a price."

"This would be the decision making and risk management tool for individuals. A life companion, the smart and wise source of information and council we all could have used at some point. How does it compare to the free version?"

"The free version is pure online communication, similar to all the other experiences, be it browsing the web, be it using a social network site. This is the mass product for the mass market."

"Sol, remember when I stated my objectives, one year ago? I see that you provide equality to all users who want to use it. If they have a smartphone or a tablet with Internet access, they can use it for free. I like that. Let us go back to the interface. How does a user phrase his questions, his situation, his dreams, his hopes, and fears, and how does he receive the answer? It has to be simple; otherwise people might not want to use it."

Sol activated his notebook and faced it towards Mr. Goodwill. On the notebook screen, a person appeared and asked how it can be of help.

"Mr. Goodwill, this is the textured face of my dad. He passed away many years ago. I did not have any recordings of his voice so I was unable to mimic his voice. This is the standalone application, the personal avatar mentor. It works with voice recognition software so you can talk and the application will do its task based on what you tell it to do. It will ask you all the questions it needs to know in order to process the situation, analyze all the variables, and eventually provide you with council. The personal avatar mentor is similar to an interaction with a wise person. You can have any face and voice you like. It is all based on personal preferences. This standalone application can provide very detailed analysis, very comprehensive council, and because it is yours, it stores the history of your interaction. Both the personal avatar mentor and the free version do the same basic thing. They help the person make decisions. What should I do will no longer be a very lonely question. Let's go to the restaurant and test the smartphone version!"

What Are My Odds?

The Institute's restaurant was rather busy, and Sol knew that it was the proper setting for the first demonstration of the free version of the database.

"Mr. Goodwill, our restaurant is the closest thing we have to a pub or club where young can socialize. My teenage daughter sometimes dreams of becoming an actress. We spend some time going through that topic, and she realized that her chances are very vague. You know how young people are, life is in front of them, and they believe that anything is possible. But they have no clue about what it takes, and how much time and effort it may require. In most cases, they do not realize that their present dream is nothing but a dream. Let us imagine that we are in a club, surrounded by young people, and we are just like them. And I am a young lady while you are making a pass at me, telling me that I could be a great actress just if I devote my time to you. Let's consult the database using our smartphone."

Sol activated the database app and a starting screen showed up. Choosing from the menu, he clicked on career counseling. The app provided a list of questions that it needed in order to provide council. Sol answered the imaginary questions of own age, gender, residence, talents, and a dozen more questions. After having answered a series of questions, the screen on his smartphone showed some numbers.

"You see Mr. Goodwill, I asked the Optimism Database to help me out with your story. What it tells me is that in principle, the chances for me to become a popular and successful actress are about 0.000000007 %. This is based on the information I have provided. It is not a perfect answer, but it comes close to the real odds."

Mr. Goodwill looked at Sol's smartphone and started to laugh.

"If I had been the young gentleman promising a successful career as an actress to a young lady I just met in a club, I guess the smartphone would tell her that I am a genuine liar. Do all people understand what the odds really mean?"

"We looked into it. There are several ways how one can present the information, so the user can easily understand it. The odds for something to happen, something to be true, or to simply have a theoretical chance of some success can be presented as percentage points, as in the case of the actress question. It can be presented as odds 1: whatever, say, 1:110 or 1:200.000.000. If the user wants it even simpler or has problems with understanding numbers, we borrowed from a child's game and devised an interface which conveys the odds, the chances of something happening or not, in terms of hot and cold. Hot is presented with a red color and cold with a white color. Depending upon the quality of the gadget screen, the colors that answer the question can provide a good guideline to the user for understanding the likely outcome of the situation."

"Yes Sol, that makes sense. Some people have trouble understanding numbers. As I understand it, this brief demonstration shows that the decision making tool, being the Optimism Database, can help the user cope with many situations. He who wants to can start focusing on those venues and paths in life where his chances are the best!"

"Exactly so Mr. Goodwill, the user can make own choices, the database is just a tool, it makes no choices for the user. Mr. Max wanted to demonstrate the system to you in his office, addressing more refined scenarios. Perhaps you care to join him and discuss the potentials of the system?"

The Price of Disillusionment

Mr. Goodwill and Mr. Max sat at the big round conference table in the executive office of the Institute. It was snowing outside. Mr. Max offered refreshments to his client before talking about business.

"Mr. Goodwill, we agreed one year ago that we will share resources, and that the Institute is interested to participate in whatever business model we create for you. I must admit that as the project developed, I became more aware of the potential it has. Are you familiar with the five stages of grief?"

"Max, you mean the Kübler-Ross model which deals with the five stages of grief initiated by a a major traumatic event?"

"Yes, that's the model. A major traumatic event can be many things. A small to medium sized business going bankrupt will have traumatic consequences for many families, and the society will lose incomes of the people affected. More than that, there is a real potential for additional traumas. Monetary losses, restrictions imposed on the welfare system, hardships, families breaking apart, and many more. I was thinking about the true cost of disillusionment which is never mentioned. Do you remember what the five stages of grief are?"

"Yes I do: Denial, anger, bargaining, depression, and acceptance are the five stages of grief. A person, actually, a company, a society too, will first deny, than be angry, then try to somehow bargain, then enter a depressive phase before it eventually accepts that whatever happened has happened. Only after acceptance can one move forward. It is a painful and time consuming process. I went through it twice."

Mr. Max felt that the conversation was leading towards the envisaged objective of both parties understanding that, apart from philanthropist motives, there was also business potential in the product. Mr. Max continued with his sales pitch.

"I know that most will say that life is a series of experiences, and that we have to make mistakes in order to learn from them. But, we tend to forget what we learned and societies in general forget even faster. When you stated your objectives one year ago, I realized that there is a potential to tackle the real question of why the world is as it is, whether we can do something to change it, and whether it can be financed. You asked for a free product, and during our creative phase we learned that we can accommodate more than we initially had hoped for. If you wish to give to the people, it somehow has to be sustainable. There has to be some revenue somewhere. Otherwise it will have a nice start and just when everyone starts to use it, the money is gone. I have identified side effects

196

of what we created for you. I am interested in our participation in the product, all the way!"

Mr. Goodwill felt good about what he seen till now and was more and more comfortable with the proposal of the Institute's chairman.

"Mr. Max, I am pleased that the creative process identified more than I have hoped for. What are the side effects that you mentioned?"

"The five stages of grief address many situations in life. The time spent in these five stages can be of a very long duration. People get disillusioned all the time, and the process of grievance is usually unproductive. Often the disillusioned person missed out on lifesaving opportunities along the way. The Optimism Database can help both individuals as well small businesses avoid certain illusions or even identify the illusions imposed by society."

"Give me an example, Mr. Max, how can the Optimism Database help people avoid the trap of illusions? An example of something that is important and relevant, please."

"Mr. Goodwill, the same product that we provided to your trillion dollar investment fund, packaged lightly, for the people and the small business communities can help avoid major traumatic events that have tragic consequences. For example, people thinking about buying a property may check with the Optimism Database what the actual real odds are that something will go wrong. They get an unbiased opinion provided by seasoned financial advisers and aided by the power of a supercomputer. Do you think that the people who are now homeless and who most likely will not recover, would have purchased properties on credit during the recent real estate boom? Had they known that there are real dangers and a high likelihood that things will go wrong, would they have purchased properties that are now underwater?"

Mr. Goodwill smiled and replied.

"Some would have, some people do not care about expert opinion at all. But, had many of the victims had someone trustworthy whom they could have asked, someone who could have explained the situation in some simple format, then the situation would have been different."

"You see Mr. Goodwill, we learned during the creative phase of this project that the database can help people and small businesses master many different situations in life. Just like with our products for the corporate world, the principle is the same. We can tell people and small businesses what the real chances are that something may or may not happen. We can calculate the most likely outcomes to almost any situation. This is what the Optimism Database can do."

Mr. Goodwill asked for more coffee and started to make calculations in his head. His business senses were hyper active.

"I see that you mention small businesses as well. This is good because small businesses employ so many people and are endangered in the corporate world of today. It is a fact that the vast majority of people have to work to survive; it is all interconnected. Well done, Mr. Max, very well done!"

Mr. Max served the client a fresh cup of coffee and mimicked the approach of a class waiter in a class restaurant.

"Mr. Goodwill, the database can serve the people, the small businesses and much more, in a reliable fashion. Some of the capabilities have to be sold for money in order to make as much of the wisdom available to everyone, for free. I took the liberty and talked with many experts on various affairs. As stated, we now have the starting 108 mentors on standby. Just in the domain of financial counseling, we have more than 200 independent consultants who are willing to provide their expertise through the database – and for much less money than when working for clients in person. Consultants would work from home, and yet they see benefits of making personal revenue. You know, separately from Sol's global opinion poll, I conducted my own opinion poll. I asked all the associates and consultants who work for our Institute whether they would provide their expertise through the database. We have more than two thousand prime quality brains that work with us from time to time. More than two thirds responded that they would be interested to interact with the database as potential mentors. Therefore, on the side of the wisdom, there is huge potential. Our own supercomputer can handle the task, so that is not an issue either. There are real business as well real philanthropist objectives that are reachable."

"Mr. Max, I will ask you what your project manager asked me one year ago. How can the database benefit the users, above all, the people?"

Mr. Max anticipated such a question and pressed a button beneath the table. On the 60-inch LCD screen statements started to scroll:

-       Users will increase their chances to focus on those things, actions, and venues in life that may provide positive results.

-       Usage of the Optimism Database lessens the exposure to predicaments that are directly resulting from immature, naïve, and hasty actions.

-       The increase in the number of relatively successful and content people will have positive impact on society as a whole.

-       The number of Internet savvy youths is dramatically increasing and the availability of electronic gadgets as well wireless communications are also increasing. While there is a lot of knowledge based content available to the user, there is a clear niche to help the young generations become wiser.

-       Wisdom is acquired by just a small number of people, and it takes decades to acquire it. Our creation foresees that there is a technological
199

way of both accelerating the time required to reach certain levels of wisdom as well increasing the number of people who seek wisdom. Because one cannot foretell how many young people would actually want to become wiser, and how many of them really understand what wisdom is, we looked into some very conservative figures.

-        If 0.5 % (one in two hundred) of the youth embark on the path of seeking and obtaining wisdom per year, by 2035 when the Optimism Database would celebrate its 10th anniversary of going online, humanity would have a least 100 million people who have reached at least some level of wisdom before their 40th birthday. This provides for sufficient critical mass.

-        If by 2035 the world has those 100 million wise people, regardless of hierarchical models in place and the problems humanity faces, sufficient wisdom would be introduced in all regions of the world and all aspects of life. All fields of interest would benefit from the accelerated trend of spreading wisdom.

Mr. Goodwill understood the message. Mr. Max handed the client a set of two USB sticks with the complete file of the product. All calculations, different business plans with numerous options, listing of companies, institutions and universities that have expressed interest to participate in the creation and roll-out of the Optimism Database and various blue-prints and diagrams – all of the work the Institute did in the twelve months of the year 2018 were handed over to the client.

The Opticase

Before the meeting ended, Mr. Goodwill asked about the contents of the small suitcase that stood in the middle of the conference table. Mr. Max stood up, took the suitcase and walked to Mr. Goodwill. He opened the suitcase to show its content and explained what it was.

"My dear friend, we looked into many options on how to provide something useful to any group of people who might face the challenge of living in a world conceived to be much different than today. After many prototypes, we opted for this small composite made suitcase. It is durable, it is hardened, it can float, and it contains a low powered computer, durable batteries, extendable solar panels, a dynamo which can recharge the batteries by hand and all components are replaceable. You even have a reserve monitor, keyboard, and solar panel packed inside of this one. We call it the Opticase because the one who owns it can be an Optimist, given all the knowledge packed into it. It contains in 50 languages all the knowledge accumulated in the past several thousands of years. It contains diagrams, how-to-do manuals, and texts that address everything one needs to know. We negotiated with major manufacturers and provide you with the prices for batches of 1,000, 10,000 and 100,000 of them. Given the fact that you will be spending a significant amount of money on the database, you may want to introduce the Opticase to the markets as a high-end gadget. There are sufficient numbers of people who believe that they should prepare themselves for the doomsday scenario and can pay for a gadget like this. I know that you will give away the Opticase to schools on all six continents. Perhaps you can give away more of everything by making some income from those who can afford it? This is our present to you. Thank you for your business, Mr. Goodwill."

The client was honored and satisfied. He paid for one and received two products.

The grandchildren

During the following two days, Mr. Goodwill was preoccupied with the testing of both products. The Institute provided a real time mock-up of the database with a team of 108 mentors lead by Professor Wunderberg, being available around the clock. The Institute's supercomputer did its role in providing facilitation of the proper mentor as well learning in due process and expanding the future database which, at one point in the not so distant future, was expected to work autonomously.

Mr. Goodwill could be seen throwing the Opticase into the nearby creek and the Institute's interns would do their best to fish it out of the cold water. They even had to search the bottom of a cliff for a whole day before they could find it after Mr. Goodwill released the Opticase from a hundred meters into the abyss.

The client was so thrilled with the Optimism Database that he ordered his grandchildren to be flown in to join the testing of it. The grandchildren were especially pleased and confirmed that the idea was sound, understandable, and will be used by those who need wisdom – the young generations to whom we hand over an endless pile of problems simply because we and our ancestors did not practice sufficient wisdom during our lifetimes.

On the 24th day of December 2018, Mr. Goodwill departed onboard his corporate jet.

It will be interesting to see how the Optimism Database will be used once it is brought online, and what effect it will have on the users. Hopefully the Opticase will never be needed. But these are some other stories to be told at a later date.

THE END